other chapter thus began in the long debate over federal aid to education, the relationship between public and church-connected schools, and the broader issue of the place of religion in the public school curriculum, which from time to time has agitated many communities. This book presents a pertinent synopsis of the background of these issues together with statements from scholars and educators representing various points of view.

Summaries of the present legal position and of historical antecedents are followed by essays by a Presbyterian, a Lutheran, a Catholic, a Reform Jew, and an advocate of the humanist view. A chapter is devoted to shared-time programs, and such questions as joint holiday observances, the common-core curriculum, the child-benefit theory are evaluated in these essays. Finally, in the A.A.S.A. report, the place of religion in the schools is discussed in both theoretical and practical terms. An appendix gives the results of a survey of actual practice in Indiana.

DAVID W. BEGGS, III, and R. BRUCE McQUIGG are faculty members of the School of Education at Indiana University. Mr. Beggs is co-editor of the *Bold New Venture* series.

AMERICA'S
SCHOOLS
AND
CHURCHES
Partners in Conflict

AMERICA'S SCHOOLS AND CHURCHES

Partners in Conflict

•

Edited by
DAVID W. BEGGS, III
R. BRUCE McQUIGG

INDIANA UNIVERSITY PRESS
Bloomington & London

ACKNOWLEDGMENTS

Special credit must be given to the outstanding contributors, whose combined energies provided the materials from which the editors shaped this book. No single author could hope to marshal ideas with the range of views offered in these collective essays.

Chapter 13, "Accommodations to Religious Pluralism," is taken in its entirety from the 1964 report by the Commission on Religion in the Public Schools of the American Association of School Administrators. We are grateful to the A.A.S.A. for permission to use this material from their publication, *Religion in the Public Schools*.

If there are gaps in the range of contemporary views on the subject examined here, the fault rests with the editors. Because of space limitations and possible duplication, we were necessarily selective in choosing material, and several excellent essays could not be included.

Appreciation must be expressed to our wives, Joan McQuigg and JoAnn Beggs, who were patient and encouraging as this book was put together. Their advice and consultation were invaluable.

Particular gratitude is due to Miriam S. Farley, Susan Fernandez, and John P. Dessauer of the Indiana University Press, who wore the hats of constructive critics, as well as editorial craftsmen.

Peter and Pamela Casagrande, who read the manuscript and made valuable editorial suggestions, were very much appreciated. Pat Stapleton handled the typing chores. Finally, we cannot neglect to thank the teachers, ministers, priests, rabbis, and students who helped shape the views we hold.

DAVID W. BEGGS, III
R. BRUCE McQUIGG

Bloomington, Indiana
October, 1965

CONTENTS

PREFACE

Two Supreme Court decisions in 1963[1] were important milestones in a long and sometimes heated debate over the proper place of religion in the public schools. The Court's finding that, in the cases before it, reading of the Bible in public schools is unconstitutional gave rise to a controversy that has not yet abated. Some lauded the decisions as upholding the basic democratic principle of separation of church and state; others, fearing a weakening of religion, called for a constitutional amendment to nullify the Court's decisions.

A related question, also discussed in this book, is whether it is possible to teach *about* religion in courses in history, literature, and the like, without falling into the trap of sectarian prejudice. Other issues of church-state relations are similarly controversial, notably that of using tax funds to aid, directly or indirectly, private schools, including those sponsored by religious bodies. The federal education act of 1965[2] opened up new possibilities of accommodation between divergent views on this issue.

1. The *Engel* and *Schempp* cases, discussed on pages 20, 29-33.
2. See pages 45-47.

The current debate over the relationships between America's schools and her churches reveals much confusion and deep concern, for the questions at issue involve fundamental differences of belief about the nature of man, the purpose of life, and the functions of education and of the churches. It is not the purpose of this book to attempt definitive treatment of these underlying issues, or to present any neat solutions to complex problems. Rather, as an aid to intelligent discussion, we present in brief compass highlights of the legal and historical background of current issues together with a representative selection of differing viewpoints and some practical suggestions. Because of this wide diversity of views, it would be well at this point for us, as editors, to offer a few remarks about the contributors and the reasons they were selected as spokesmen.

Homer P. Rainey, an experienced administrator, points to the divided opinion on many issues, the confusion about policy and practice among educators, and the difficulty in interpreting the First Amendment to the Constitution. These undercurrents of controversy form the basis of the questions discussed in the course of this book.

Natt Burbank was superintendent of schools during a highly turbulent period in one community. His first-person account vividly illustrates the problems an educator sometimes faces, and he outlines precautionary measures against such community conflict.

Both the review of important court cases pertaining to religion and education in America, by David M. Cook, an Indianapolis lawyer, and the historical summary of some significant developments in education from the time of the nation's beginnings, by the editors, give the reader essential background for understanding the complexity of the religion-education issues.

Although Chapters Five through Nine are written by representatives of various sects or philosophical positions, they do not purport to speak for all members of these sects. By reviewing and interpreting in the light of the religion-education dilemma some aspects of Presbyterian theology, Theron B. Maxson discusses the Presbyterian record of support of the public schools. Dr. Arthur L. Miller's explanation of the Lutheran views, on the other hand, expresses the need for church-related schools and shows the position of the Lutheran Church-Missouri Synod.

Robert F. Drinan, S.J. examines the Catholic Church's position toward federal aid to education. He also discusses what he terms "the release of education to the state by Protestant bodies" and cites the "pan-Protestant" orientation in our public schools.

By his clarifying explanation of the basic tenets of Reform Judaism, Rabbi Alexander M. Schindler reveals the Jewish view of education. He also questions the value of joint holiday observances (Christmas-Hanukkah) and of a common-core, nondenominational religious curriculum.

Stanley E. Ballinger considers from the humanist angle the myriad problems in teaching *about* religion. He offers some pertinent insights on what he calls "countervailing principles of free inquiry and cultural inclusiveness."

The controversial subject of prayer and Bible-reading in the schools is treated by Dean M. Kelley. He suggests that the public school's responsibility toward religion is instructional rather than devotional, and he deplores what he terms "low-demand religion."

The suggested solution of shared time is reviewed by Melvin P. Heller from the administrative side of the fence. He offers several considerations that administrators must recognize and solve if they are to successfully implement shared-time programs.

From a position outside any specific interest group, J. Renwick Jackson emphasizes the value of dialogue and the process by which diverse views "harmonize" into a public philosophy, and ultimately the importance of the ministry of the laity to bring this harmony about.

While certainly not conclusive, a book which brings together various viewpoints will, it is hoped, be helpful to practicing educators, both teachers and administrators, to church members both lay and clerical, to members of school boards and legislatures, and to other interested citizens.

"America's schools," as used in the title of the book, refers to elementary and secondary schools only. The problems of higher education receive only peripheral mention.

The term "parochial school" has different meanings for different people. Often it is used as a synonym for Catholic elementary and secondary schools, whether administered by a parish, a diocese, or a religious order. In this book we have followed Webster's definition of "a school maintained by a religious body."

"Released time" and "shared time" refer to two methods of cooperation between school and church that have been practiced in various communities. "Released time" typically refers to a situation in which children are released from the public school during certain periods in order to receive religious instruction provided by their own churches off the school premises. In "shared time" parochial school children are permitted to enroll in public school classes for part of their instruction, usually in the more technical subjects.

DAVID W. BEGGS, III
R. BRUCE McQUIGG

AMERICA'S
SCHOOLS
AND
CHURCHES
Partners in Conflict

Chapter One

•

INTRODUCTION

HOMER P. RAINEY

Religion's place in the public schools is one of the continuing problems in American education. It is highly controversial because of the range of religious pluralism in the United States and the widely differing opinions of the numerous religious groups. Testimony supporting this contention appears in Chapter Two of this book.

Quite likely the solution to the problem will be a more difficult one for our society than the problem of racial segregation. There is fair consensus that racial segregation violates the human rights of democratic citizenship. While this opinion has been confirmed by a unanimous decision of the Supreme Court of the United States, there is no consensus about many of the issues involving religious liberty and the separation of church and state. In fact, the Supreme Court has been divided by five to four on several decisions. And the court has actually re-

Homer P. Rainey is a Professor Emeritus of Education at the University of Colorado. He has been the President of Franklin College, Stephens College, and the University of Texas.

3

versed itself in the famous Flag Salute case, discussed below. There are many instances in which state supreme courts have disagreed with the United States Supreme Court and with each other. For example, in the matter of reading the Bible in school the states are divided into four nearly equal groups with respect to what they require and what they will permit. Until the Supreme Court handed down its clarifying decisions in 1962 and 1963, one group of states allowed, and their courts even encouraged, reading and discussing the Bible in the public schools. Another group allowed Bible reading but disapproved of discussions of the book in a religious context. The third group of states approved the use of the Bible by students on a voluntary basis. The fourth group ruled that study of the Bible, with or without comment and even on a voluntary basis, was inappropriate in the public schools. The same confusion exists with regard to many other issues related to education and religion, such as released time, prayers at opening exercises, religious holiday celebrations, and so forth.

Diversity of opinion persists on what the First Amendment to the Constitution of the United States really means when applied to the role of religion in the public schools. The issues are still unresolved, even after generations of litigation. The intent of the First Amendment was twofold: (a) to prohibit any established religion in the United States, and (b) to guarantee complete religious liberty. These purposes when applied to public schools sometimes are found to be in conflict. Pertinent questions continue to be asked. What constitutes worship? What is sectarian instruction? Do public financial contributions to nonpublic schools constitute support of religion? Can religious freedom endure if religion is kept from the schools?

There are several recent pointed examples of this disagreement. The flag salute cases are one. Pennsylvania law required children in the schools to salute the flag. The Jehovah's Witnesses opposed this requirement and challenged it in the courts of Pennsylvania in the case of the Minersville School District. The court of first hearing was upheld by the other Pennsylvania courts and then by the United States Supreme Court. But later a similar case (the *Barnette* case) came through the West Virginia courts and on to the United States Supreme Court, which reversed the West Virginia state courts. The high court took a broad, long-range view in its decision and expressed new sensitivity to the minority rights of the Jehovah's Witnesses and others who are opposed to any religious influence in the public schools. "No official . . . can prescribe what shall be orthodox in politics, nationalism, religion . . . or force citizens to confess by word or action their faith therein."[1] In other words a citizen cannot be forced to salute the flag so long as the objection is a matter of religious conviction.

Another good example of the shift in view is the famous *McCollum* case involving released time. Illinois schools permitted released time for religious instruction. When Mrs. McCollum challenged it, the Illinois courts sustained the practice. In 1948 the United States Supreme Court reversed the Illinois courts and declared this practice unconstitutional.[2]

Such evidence indicates that there is much confusion throughout the nation among the leaders of public education about policies and practices in this highly controversial area. Educational practices vary widely from state to state and from community to community. The recent study of Indiana school practices reported in the Appendix of this book documents this diversity. School executives are sometimes timid and hesitant to undertake programs of any kind that involve the relations of religion to public education. At other times educators hesitate to interfere with traditional school practices, even after the

Supreme Court has spoken. Teachers are uncertain about how to handle matters of religion in the schools, and all the possible legal interpretations are not clear to them.

In recent years there have been countless attempts to solve these problems. Practically every major church group in the nation has passed resolutions on these issues. The National Council of Churches has had a commission working on the problems for some time, and the Greater Federation of Churches in the Chicago area has authorized a similar group. Similarly, educational groups, such as the American Council on Education and the American Association of School Administrators, have made lengthy studies and issued significant reports making detailed recommendations about these relationships. Also there have been many similar state and local committees. The National Council of Churches and the American Association of School Administrators cosponsored a conference on these problems. But still the controversy continues. One significant chapter of the 1964 American Association of School Administrators' report, *Religion in the Public Schools*, is included as Chapter Thirteen of this book.

Several major proposals for dealing with this problem of religion in the schools have resulted. In one of the earlier proposals Dean Luther Weigle of the Yale Divinity School, speaking in behalf of the National Council of Churches, suggested that the various religious groups get together and agree upon a common core of materials on religion to be taught in the schools. No agreement could be reached and this suggestion never was implemented.

The American Council on Education, after a number of years of study, recommended that the schools "teach about religion," a practice which is rather widely used in the study of literature, art, and history. Although some contend it is the best approach to this problem, more interest is expressed in the "teach about religion" theory in the Southern and Midwestern parts of the country than in the Eastern and Western sections.

The Educational Policies Commission of the National Education Association recommended the teaching of moral and spiritual values in public schools. This approach has been implemented, and some states even require such teaching by state law. The subject is discussed in some detail throughout this book.

The practice of released time gained wide support until the United States Supreme Court decision in the *McCollum* case. No separation exists between church and state, the high court said, so long as a single worship practice or any systematic indoctrination are regular parts of any school program.

More recently a shared-time plan has aroused considerable discussion and some experimentation. This proposal is rather recent and we do not have enough experience for a final judgment on it at this time. While there is considerable support for the idea, there are also many administrative problems involved in its application. Chapter Eleven discusses this approach to the problem.

Why is there controversy and confusion about these issues? Are religion and public education antagonistic? During the colonial period of our history, education and religion were closely related. Education was sponsored and supported largely by religious groups, and the curricula of schools were predominantly religious and moral in orientation. This, of course, was before the nation committed itself to extensive free tax-supported public schools. This was a period when our society was not really pluralistic. When a new stage of our history was reached in the period between 1830 and 1860, various new problems arose. And for the last hundred years every state and almost every school district in the nation has been wrestling with the role of religion in education.

The problem is further complicated by our political ideal of religious liberty and our hazy notion of the doctrine of the separation of church and state. What do these principles mean with respect to the teaching of religion and religious practices in the public schools? We have gone through a long history of evolution of church-state relationships, from the theocratic state, in which the state and the church were one, to the development of the concept of a free church in a free state. Federal and state constitutions have strong provisions providing for what Thomas Jefferson called "a wall of separation between church and state." What these constitutions provide for is religious liberty. But what constitutes a violation of the separation is not clear. Religious liberty has five conditions. It is unconstitutional to pass any law (1) relating to an establishment of religion; (2) compelling support, by taxation or otherwise, of religious instruction; (3) compelling attendance at religious worship; (4) restraining the free exercise of religion according to the dictates of one's own conscience; and (5) restraining the expression of religious belief. The implementation of these principles through court decisions has resulted in the elimination of many former practices of the public schools and has added greatly to increasing concern about the relations of religion and public education.

This relationship is further complicated by the widely held opinion that education that does not include religion is only partial, incomplete, or wholly inadequate. Pope Pius XI expressed this idea in his encyclical on *The Christian Education of Youth*, in which he said: "There can be no ideally perfect education which is not Christian education."

The nature and purposes of the public schools in this country are such that it has been found necessary to eliminate sectarianism and sectarian instruction. This has been a very difficult process, partly because of a lack of agreement concerning just what constitutes sectarian instruction. For example, does reading the Bible (the King James version) constitute sectarian instruction? Does the wearing of a distinctive religious garb constitute sectarian influence? Does the singing of psalms and hymns and the reciting of prayers make the school a place of worship? These questions draw different answers from different people. As the composition of communities has changed, differences have arisen even where agreement once existed.

If no constitutional changes are made, it seems fairly clear that we shall have to accept the concept of a secular public school system. Instruction in religion or religious exercises is not a function of the public schools; hence it must be assumed by the home and the church.

On the other hand, if some constitutional change should be adopted, then the whole matter will have to be reviewed. Corresponding readjustments will have to be made. Specifically, the adoption of the Becker Amendment (whereby reading the Bible and reciting prayers would be legalized) or some similar constitutional change would throw out every state and Supreme Court decision regarding the relation of religion and the public schools. It would cast doubts on the clauses of every state constitution which guarantee religious liberty. It would invalidate every state law in the fifty states which prohibits the teaching of religion, the reading of the Bible, the offering of prayers, and so forth. Almost unimaginable chaos would result. If the latter alternative is adopted, the American public is going to be forced to make a reevaluation of religion and the public schools in the context of American tradition and contemporary beliefs. This reevaluation will involve discussion of some of the most basic concepts of the American heritage of religious liberty and the delicate relation of church and state.

Chapter Two

•

REASON VERSUS EMOTION
IN A COMMUNITY

NATT B. BURBANK

Burning fitfully in front of the home of the superintendent of schools, a rude cross symbolized the height of emotion which had built up in a Colorado community torn by controversy over religion in the schools in the 1960's. Friend turned against friend, church memberships divided into opposite camps, civic organizations split down the middle in argument, and the public school teachers took sides.

On the lips of nearly everyone were questions about religious and educational issues. Letters swamped the press with impetuous opinions based more on emotion than on reason. People said and did things which they would never have considered under normal circumstances. Level-headed citizens were elbowed aside in the general emotional stampede to be heard.

Dr. Burbank is Associate Professor of Education at Lehigh University. In addition to teaching at the University of Maine and Western State College in Colorado, he was Superintendent of Schools in Boulder, Colorado for fifteen years. Dr. Burbank was President of the American Association of School Administrators in 1963-64.

Finally when a crowd of young hoodlums burned a cross on the lawn of the superintendent, the community realized that it was on an emotional binge. The cross-burning triggered a wave of revulsion among the reasonable people of the city. When the Board of Education calmly and thoughtfully organized a strong citizens' committee a few weeks later, people from all walks of life and with all shades of opinion on the issue began to take stock of what had been happening.

This capsule account of six to eight weeks of torment in one contemporary American city is not fiction. Other towns in recent years have experienced similar crises over questions of religion and education. Not always does the controversy reach such a climax, but the same type of emotional flight from reason usually characterizes these outbursts.

Few if any issues rend a school system and community as deeply as does the religious question. Neither immorality nor disloyalty of public employees fires such righteous indignation. Diverse elements of the community are attracted to the same banner of emotionalism. Though some are strange companions, together they compose a big army.

Muddled Issues

More often than not when communities become involved in conflict on the problem of religion and the schools, the basic issues are largely forgotten. Mounting emotions warp reason until fundamental questions are submerged and unimportant issues stay at the surface.

Often this situation can be charged to the ineptness of school leaders. Lack of sensitivity to public opinion sometimes blinds administrators and school board members to the rapidly rising tide of conflict. The reaction of the author in such a situation was one of reluctance to enter into public argument over this critical question. It seemed best to say as little as possible in the hope that the trouble would dissolve. While this may happen in some cases, more often positive action is urgently needed. Hindsight frequently indicates clearly what should have been done.

In the city described the original issue was the amount of school time to be devoted to rehearsing for Christmas pageants. Originally it was a school rather than a religious issue. In their enthusiasm for their fields of specialization, the music and art teachers had been requiring more and more time for their preparations for the Christmas pageants. During the last two weeks of school before the Christmas presentations, an unwarranted amount of class time was lost because of rehearsals.

The school board and the administration acted to reduce the amount of time thus taken away from academic pursuits. In most of the schools of the city, principals and teachers loyally and fully complied with directives. However, in a few cases the teachers of music and art rebelled at the inroads made upon their preparation period for the Christmas programs. They advised their students to tell their parents that the school board and superintendent were moving to take Christmas out of the schools. At this point the situation caught the attention of the community, which moved with lightning swiftness. Within forty-eight hours the situation was completely out of hand. Almost at once the paramount issue in the minds of many citizens was whether there were atheism and Communism in the schools. Eliminating class time spent on rehearsals for a Christmas program was translated into an attack on Christianity.

At no time had the school board and the administration intended to remove the singing of Christmas carols from the schools. There was no thought of ruling out religious themes in art classes or eliminating the appropriate study of religious history. Yet all of these charges were leveled and they were widely believed.

In the local newspaper letters to the editor, normally limited to two columns, were filling a complete page day after day. Many of these letters contained extreme statements which were so far from the truth that they would have been laughable under less chaotic conditions.

In community conflicts people with differing motives sometimes take the same side for varied and often incongruous reasons. In disputes over the role of religion in education, the diversity of motivation is especially wide. In this Colorado community, the division within churches, civic organizations, and other social institutions produced deep-seated wounds which healed slowly.

Some of those who advocated including religion in the school program were conscientious and devout men and women, many of them staunch church members, who believed that if the schools do not teach religious theory and precept, they will be encouraging the cause of atheism. Others though, more nominal than practicing Christians, were prompted to ally themselves with this side of the controversy. Some bewailed the moral deterioration of the schools, while others related the issue to the influence of Communism.

Disorganized but equally vociferous was the coterie of people who held grudges against the schools or against individuals in the school system. Some of these crusaders adopted the crisis as a substitute for the issue they had been unable to find. Others in this group were merely excitement-seekers, who clustered along the fringes, interested only in the turmoil.

In the same camp were the citizens who dared not take a stand against the mob. They meant well but found it impossible to stand up for what they felt to be right. They went along without bitterness, sometimes even apologetically, but still they went along.

The power of the anti-separation forces stemmed from the

collective motivations of most of these groups: the devout churchmen, the nominal Christians, the thrill-seekers, and the yes-men. Whatever their aims and objectives, the composite result of their effort became a tornado of passion.

Diversity was found also in the ranks of the supporters of separation of religion and education. Many of them were level-headed, quiet people with a strong desire to return to normalcy. They wanted school time used for the basic purposes of education, and they constituted an unobtrusive force for improvement of the situation. Others took a stand for separation of religion and education because they wanted to see the church strengthened. They believed that a vigorous and effective program of religious education conducted by the church itself strengthens the position of the church, while the extent to which the schools attract community interest in religious observances proportionately weakens the church and its effect on its people.

The most controversial members of the separation forces seemed to be the atheists and agnostics. Perhaps because their rationale is little understood and tends to perplex an ordinary American community, they contributed little in this case but embarrassment to the total effort of the separation team.

Differences in belief about the role of religion in education can be found not only between but even within church congregations. In this particular case the groups were split along liberal-conservative lines, the liberals supporting separation of church and state, the conservatives favoring some form of religious observance in the schools. Fundamentalist groups seemed to be unanimously in favor of religion in the schools, while at the other end of the spectrum, the Unitarian and Jewish congregations advocated total separation.

The clergy aligned themselves along the philosophical horizon from liberal to conservative. As spiritual leaders of their congregations they found themselves in a most difficult situation. Extreme pressures on them from both sides limited the chances for some of them to speak out strongly. Others managed to stand firmly for a dignified and rational analysis of the problem without attacking the integrity of those who differed with them. Most of the clergy in the latter category welcomed the retreat of schools from excessive involvement in religious seasonal activities at Christmas and Easter. They believed that religion is the responsibility of the home and the church and that the greater the involvement by the schools, the less emphasis on church leadership on religious occasions.

The assumption that a positive public statement at the outset by the schools might have prevented the situation is substantiated by the fact that less than a year later, after careful community-wide study, a school board policy was adopted which was virtually identical with the policy in effect during the crisis. The absence of criticism during three subsequent Christmas seasons indicates that this policy is well accepted by the community.

Issues related to religious freedom are often confused because of lack of knowledge of our Bill of Rights. The right of the individual to be free of duress in religion is guaranteed by the First Amendment. Some find it difficult to accept this as a reason for leaving religious exercises out of school activities. Only a thorough understanding of the spirit of the Bill of Rights can provide a sound basis for public policy on religion in education.

Preventive Measures

When fundamental issues are distorted by emotion, it is difficult for any community, however enlightened, to maintain its objectivity. A thorough and dispassionate community-wide study may well be the best possible insurance against an outburst over the question of religion and education. While there is a certain amount of risk in bringing up such a controversial subject, there is a greater possibility of a successful outcome when men of good will sit down to study the problem in the absence of any specific controversy. Once the emotions of individuals and groups are aroused, it is too late for rational discussion.

In a city-wide attack upon the problems of religion and education it is imperative that every shade of religious philosophy be included in the group. Catholics, Jews, fundamentalists, middle-of-the-roaders, liberal Protestants, and the unchurched should all be represented, as should varying political and economic philosophies. An essential qualification for membership in such a group should be a willingness to listen to the beliefs of others.

Before undertaking the recruitment of a committee or commission to analyze the issues, it would be well to lay the groundwork carefully. Informal consultation with community leaders such as clergymen, school board and city council members, and any other people who have demonstrated leadership would be desirable. It is especially desirable to have the general support of ministers and priests before the first step is taken.

Undoubtedly the most critical step in the process of setting up a study group is the selection of its leader. With a strong, fair-minded, and clear-thinking chairman, there is a good prospect of success; without such a person there is little or none. Most desirable for this post is a citizen of recognized stature in the community, one who is known for his fairness and courage, one who is respected by virtually everyone.

It is better not to include office-holders such as city council and school board members in such a study group. Their very presence places them in a position which may well compromise their freedom of action upon the recommendations of the committee. It is better to choose citizens for their individual, personal capabilities rather than their political or organizational affiliation.

Such a committee must employ legal counsel to guide them on complex legal and constitutional questions. The advice of an attorney is also needed by a board of education which finds itself involved in a religious controversy. With the help of a good lawyer, a board can avoid mistakes which would compound the problems of the hour.

The People Must Be Kept Informed

Complete press and radio coverage should be provided so that the people of the town can keep abreast of the thinking of the committee. This will minimize the likelihood of an explosion when the final report appears. If the community has not had a chance to follow the work of the committee, major groups may be shocked by the recommendations. If, on the other hand, the people have observed the developing thought of the study group, there is a more favorable climate for understanding and acceptance of the product.

The findings of the committee should be distributed throughout the town so that public and private discussion can be encouraged. Committee members should make themselves available as resource people for such deliberations. It is especially important that school-connected organizations, such as parent-teachers associations, devote considerable time to analyzing the recommendations.

One of the prerequisites for the success of an enterprise of this nature is a thorough orientation of public school employees, especially administrators and teachers. Presumably the school board and the top level of the hierarchy of administrators will have been quietly instrumental in organizing the study. The teachers, too, must be kept informed of developments. Many people look to teachers for guidance in their thinking about the schools. A well-informed and conscientious teacher can do much to develop support for school programs. Conversely a teacher who does not know what is afoot or who suspects the worst is likely to indicate by word or expression his lack of faith in what is being done.

Care must be taken, however, not to give the appearance of brainwashing. Any attempt to indoctrinate teachers in one direction or another will inevitably arouse the opposition of many of them. Information they will welcome, but special pleading and pressure will immediately antagonize them.

In the event that trouble arises, the full facts should be given to the news media without delay. Most school leaders tend to be cautious in their relationships with press and radio. But to remain silent at a time when straightforward public utterance is needed is the worst possible course of action. The vacuum thereby created encourages the brush fire of bigotry to burst into a full-fledged conflagration. If the newsmen have not been kept informed regarding developments, even at the earliest stages, they cannot be expected to react positively. On the other hand, most news people will speak out in the community interest if they know what is going on. Complete candor with press, television, and radio reporters will predispose them to treat the questions of religion and education with integrity and objectivity.

Although community turmoil is far from the most desirable outcome of a religion-education crisis, it may be better than apathy. Yet if public spirit abounds in a community, it can be constructively channeled into thoughtful study and discussion by conscientious citizens. The precautionary measures I have outlined are the best deterrent to the sort of conflict that arose in the Colorado community described here.

Chapter Three

•

THE PRESENT LEGAL
SITUATION

DAVID M. COOK

"Congress shall make no law respecting an establishment of
religion, or prohibiting the free exercise thereof. . . ."

FIRST AMENDMENT,
CONSTITUTION OF THE UNITED STATES

With these fifteen words the First Amendment to the Constitution of the United States begins. Succeeding clauses, even
briefer, set forth the basic guarantees of freedom of speech,
freedom of the press, the right of peaceable assembly, and the
right to petition the government for a redress of grievances. In
less than five lines of printed type, forty-four words in all, the
First Amendment sets forth these six monumental guarantees of
freedom, which became such a vital part of our Bill of Rights.

We are concerned here with the first of these freedoms, free-

David M. Cook is a member of the law firm of McHale, Cook, and
Welch, Indianapolis, Indiana. In addition to participation in civic affairs
in his community, he is a member of the Board of Directors of the Indiana Civil Liberties Union.

dom of religion. Although the men who drafted our Constitution succeeded in compressing this guarantee into the concise words cited, many millions of words have been uttered and written by courts, by lawyers, and by scholars in an effort to explain fully and interpret accurately their meaning.

In June of 1963 the Supreme Court of the United States handed down its decisions in two companion cases, *Abington School District* v. *Schempp* and *Murray* v. *Curlett*. The Court held that the First Amendment was violated in the one case by the "establishment" clause of a Pennsylvania statute and in the other case by a rule of the Board of School Commissioners of the city of Baltimore, adopted pursuant to statutory authority, requiring the reading without comment at the opening of each school day of verses from the Bible and the recitation by the students in unison of the Lord's Prayer.

These cases followed by approximately one year the decision of the Court in *Engel* v. *Vitale*. The Court in this case held unconstitutional a daily procedure adopted by the Board of Regents in the state of New York directing a school district to have each class at the beginning of each school day recite aloud a special prayer formulated by the Board of Regents.

Few cases decided by the Supreme Court of the United States in its entire history have evoked so much widespread public interest and so much divided comment, not only on what the Court actually decided, but also on the reasoning underlying the decisions. Thousands of analyses, commentaries, and digests of the opinion have been widely circulated. Whereas in most cases a decision of the Supreme Court is of interest primarily to lawyers and legal scholars, in these instances not only the legal profession but also school administrators, clergymen, and countless numbers of laymen have studied the decisions, or at least excerpts from them, and have arrived at their own conclusions and interpretations.

The reactions have been extremely varied. Some people have bee.. very critical of the Court and have questioned its judgment a. ᵈ motives, accusing it of being "godless" or pro-Communist. Ot.. ᵉrs have expressed bewilderment but have reconciled themselv.. to the decisions, which they feel lay down rules which have n..w become a part of the law of the land, to be followed and respe..ᵗcd, whether one's personal views agree with those of the Court or n..ᵗ Others, and the author is in this category, have agreed fully witn ᵗhe Court, believing that it has properly interpreted the Constitut.., ᵇas provided a great bulwark for one of the fundamental freedoms gu..ʳanteed by the Bill of Rights, and has given true meaning to that ficcuc..

The Perspective

An adequate consideration of the present legal situation must refer to earlier Court decisions which form its historical background. Then we must look ahead to consider possible future developments. Before reviewing the earlier decisions, however, it is appropriate to consider the nature of our judicial process and the role of the Supreme Court in interpreting the Constitution. There is a great deal of public confusion and misunderstanding on this matter, particularly among those who are critical of the Court's decisions and who believed the Court has abused its functions by "making new law," thereby usurping some of the legislative functions of government. This criticism is both unfounded and unjustified.

Our constitutional framework rests, as it always has, on a threefold division of the functions of government among the legislative, the executive, and the judicial branch. Very early in our nation's history, under the strong leadership of Chief Justice John Marshall, the Supreme Court enunciated the doctrine of judicial supremacy. That is, the courts of the land in the determination of controversies coming before them have the power, and indeed the duty, to override actions of the legislative and executive branches when the courts determine that such actions are contrary to the Constitution, which is the supreme law of the land. Of necessity this involves an interpretation of the meaning and application of the Constitution and its various clauses. The Supreme Court, as the highest court in the land, must be the final arbiter, from whose decisions there is no further appeal.

The Supreme Court and the courts below it do not act in the abstract, but only in specific cases which necessitate a determination of the rights of the particular parties then before the court. It is not permissible for the legislative branch of government, either federal or state, when considering certain proposed legislation, to ask the Supreme Court for its advice and opinion on whether the proposed legislation is constitutional. Likewise, it is not permissible for federal or state officials of the executive branch, or for private individuals, to ask the Court for an advance interpretation or opinion on the validity of their proposed action.

How, then, do these cases come before the court? Two or more persons (and in this sense the persons may include a public body or a governmental unit as well as an individual) become involved in a controversy which ripens into a lawsuit in which the determination of their respective rights and obligations turns upon a constitutional point. In the area of religion and education a case may arise in which a taxpayer brings a lawsuit to enjoin public school officials from spending tax money for what this individual claims to be an invalid purpose. Or parents of school children may bring an action for an injunction against school officials to enjoin them from conducting certain programs in the school attended by the parents' child; or some individual may bring a lawsuit to require school officials to perform a certain act. An individual may violate some law, and when he is prosecuted for the alleged violation, he may contend that the law under which he is being prosecuted is invalid. In any of these situations a justiciable controversy arises which a court will be called upon to decide.

Under normal circumstances, each of the parties to the lawsuit will employ counsel to represent its interests and to present its case before the court. One of the essential elements of this whole judicial process is the concept that there will be two parties having adverse interests and taking opposite positions so that the most forceful arguments on both sides of the case will be effectively presented to the court. In a pluralistic society differences will never be uncommon on matters of religion and education. In addition, particularly in cases with a widespread public interest, it is very common practice for other persons not directly involved in the case, but having some special interest in the subject matter, to ask the court for permission to file a written brief as *amicus curiae*—a friend of the court—setting forth reasons why the person submitting the brief feels that the court should adopt one position or another.

The case starts as an ordinary lawsuit either in the Federal District Court of the district in which the controversy arose or perhaps in a state trial court. It wends its way slowly through an arduous course of hearings and determination by the initial court, followed by an appeal to one or more higher state courts, if it had originated in the state courts. Ultimately an appeal to the Supreme Court of the United States can be made. In most cases there is a lag of two to four years from the time the case originates until the final determination by the Supreme Court is made.

Supreme Court Significance

What is the legal significance and effect of the Supreme Court decision? In a narrow, technical sense it decides only the legal rights and obligations of the parties before it. To attempt to limit its scope to the particular case, however, is to be unrealistic and to place form above substance. Whenever the Court renders a decision, it hands down a written opinion which explains not only what the Court has decided but also the reasoning upon which the decision is based. This reasoning will ordinarily be applied automatically to all similar factual situations, at least by persons who seek legal advice on the subject. Lawyers recognize that other courts will follow the decision of the Supreme Court, knowing that if they do not, their decisions can be appealed to the Supreme Court and set aside. In other situations, where the facts are not identical but where there is a related question, the opinion of the Supreme Court will be studied and analyzed with the intent to pick out the guiding principles of law and to ascertain what decision would be applied in the similar case. Very often different lawyers will arrive at conflicting conclusions and make varied interpretations as to the application of the legal principles stated by the Court. This can pave the way for a controversy which leads to a new case ultimately coming before the Court. As case after case finds its way to the Supreme Court, the series of decisions and the reasoning applied by the Court tends to establish a pattern. Thus the controlling principles of law become more and more clearly established.

A Case by Case Review

Rather remarkably, although more than 150 years had elapsed since the adoption of the Constitution, the 1947 case of

Everson v. Board of Education[1] is believed to be the first major case arising under the establishment clause of the First Amendment. It involved a New Jersey statute authorizing local school districts to make rules and contracts for the transportation of children to and from schools and to reimburse parents for bus transportation of their children on regular buses. The law in question included a provision to pay for transportation of some children in the community to Catholic schools. The suit was filed by a local taxpayer challenging the right of the Board of Education to reimburse parents of parochial school students. The Court held that there was no violation of the First Amendment, since the state contributed no money to the schools and was only establishing a general program to help parents get their children, regardless of their religion, safely and expeditiously to and from accredited schools. However, in the course of rendering its decision the Court used some extremely significant language concerning the nature and scope of the establishment clause of the First Amendment. This language has become classic and has been cited and referred to in all of the subsequent decisions. After reviewing the colonial history and the reasons for the First Amendment, the Court said:

> The "establishment of religion" clause of the First Amendment means at least this: Neither a state nor the Federal Government can set up a church. Neither can pass laws which aid one religion, aid all religions, or prefer one religion over another. Neither can force nor influence a person to go to or to remain away from church against his will or force him to profess a belief or disbelief in any religion. No person can be punished for entertaining or professing religious beliefs or disbeliefs, for church attendance or non-attendance. No tax in any amount, large or small, can be levied to support any religious activities or institutions, whatever they may be called, or whatever form they may adopt to teach or practice religion. Neither a state nor the Federal Government can, openly or secretly, partici-

pate in the affairs of any religious organizations or groups and vice versa. In the words of Jefferson, the clause against establishment of religion by law was intended to erect "a wall of separation between Church and State."

After the decision in the *Everson* case in 1947, another action came before the Supreme Court in 1948 involving a somewhat different question but one directly related to religion and public education. This case, known as *McCollum* v. *Board of Education of Champaign County*,[2] involved a challenge to a released-time program for religious instruction carried on in the schools of Champaign, Illinois. Religious instruction classes were conducted in the school building during regular school hours by outside teachers furnished by a religious council representing the various faiths and subject to the approval and supervision of the superintendent of schools. Attendance records were kept and reported to the school authorities in the same way as for other classes, and pupils not attending the religious instruction classes were required to continue their regular secular studies. The Court held that this arrangement was in violation of the Constitutional principle of separation of church and state as expressed in the First Amendment and made applicable to the states by the Fourteenth Amendment.

It may be pointed out that the First Amendment is by its terms applicable only to the federal government, and it states that "Congress shall make no law." This is true of the entire Bill of Rights, which was conceived and adopted as a limitation upon the powers of the federal government. Nearly one hundred years later, following the Civil War, the Fourteenth Amendment to the Constitution was adopted, providing among other things that no state shall make or enforce any law which shall abridge the privileges or immunities of citizens of the United States, nor shall any state deprive any person of life, liberty, or property without due process of law, nor deny to any person within its jurisdiction the equal protection of the laws. In a long series of cases involving other issues the Court had held that the privileges or immunities of citizens and the life, liberty, and property provisions of the Fourteenth Amendment necessarily guaranteed to all citizens freedom from state action in all of the areas against which freedom from federal action was guaranteed by the First Amendment.

In the *McCollum* case the Supreme Court, relying heavily on its language in the *Everson* decision of a year earlier, concluded that the released-time program in the Champaign schools was a violation of the establishment clause. One of the major contentions advanced by the attorneys for the Champaign Board of Education was that the First Amendment was intended to forbid only government preference of one religion over another, not an impartial governmental assistance of all religions. The court flatly and firmly rejected this contention and said:

> To hold that a state cannot consistently with the First and Fourteenth Amendments utilize its public school system to aid any or all religious faiths or sects in the dissemination of their doctrines and ideals does not, as counsel urge, manifest a governmental hostility to religion or religious teachings. A manifestation of such hostility would be at war with our national tradition as embodied in the First Amendment's guaranty of the free exercise of religion. For the First Amendment rests upon the premise that both religion and government can best work to achieve their lofty aims if each is left free from the other within its respective sphere. Or, as we said in the Everson Case, the First Amendment has erected a wall between Church and State which must be kept high and impregnable.

Four years later, in 1952, a new case also concerning a released-time program, but one which was quite different in many respects from the Champaign program involved in the *McCollum* case, came before the Court. This case is known as *Zorach* v. *Clauson*[3] and involved a challenge brought by parents of certain children in the New York City school system, which had a program of released time similar to that found in cities all over the United States. This program permitted the public schools on written request of the parents to release during a school day those students who attended religious courses operated outside the school building by, and at the expense of, a duly constituted religious body. All other students remained in the classroom. In contrast to the Champaign program, the New York City program was conducted without any use of coercion by the schools to get students into the religious courses. There was no supervision by school authorities and the program was not conducted in the school building. The Court held that these differences were vital and controlling. And without in any way reversing its decision in the Champaign case, the Court held that the New York type of released-time program was constitutional. The following is perhaps the most significant paragraph of the Court's opinion:

We are a religious people whose institutions presuppose a Supreme Being. We guarantee the freedom to worship as one chooses. We make room for as wide a variety of beliefs and creeds as the spiritual needs of man deem necessary. We sponsor an attitude on the part of government that shows no partiality to any one group and that lets each flourish according to the zeal of its adherents and the appeals of its dogma. When the state encourages religious instruction or cooperates with religious authorities by adjusting the schedule of public events to sectarian needs, it follows the best of our traditions. For it then respects the religious nature of our people and accomodates the public service to their spiritual needs. To hold that it may not would be to find in the Constitution a requirement that the government show a callous indifference to religious groups. That would be preferring those who believe in no religion over those who do believe. Government may not finance religious groups nor undertake religious instruction or blend secular and sectarian education nor use secular institutions to force one or some religion on any person. But we find no constitutional requirement which makes it necessary for government to be hostile to religion and to throw its weight against efforts to widen the effective scope of religious influence. The government must be neutral when it comes to competition between sects. It may not thrust any sect on any person. It may not make a religious observance compulsory. It may not coerce anyone to attend church, to observe a religious holiday, or to take religious instruction. But it can close its doors or suspend its operations as to those who want to repair to their religious sanctuary for worship or instruction. No more than that is undertaken here.

None of these cases produced any great public reaction, and they were probably largely unnoticed except by school officials and by persons directly involved in released-time programs. Following the decision of the Court in *Zorach* v. *Clauson* there was a gap of ten years before the next major decision relating to religion and the public schools.

The next major decision occurred when the case of *Engel* v. *Vitale*[4] came before the Court in 1962. The issue arose out of a procedure adopted by the Board of Education of a school district in New York State on the recommendation of the State Board of Regents. They drafted and approved a short, simple twenty-three-word prayer reading as follows:

Almighty God, we acknowledge our dependence upon Thee, and we beg Thy blessings upon us, our parents, our teachers and our country.

This prayer, obviously designed to be an interdenominational or nondenominational formula which might be acceptable to all faiths, was required to be said aloud by each class in the presence of the teacher at the beginning of each school day. The parents of certain pupils brought action challenging the constitutionality of both the state law and the school district's regulation ordering the recitation of the particular prayer.

After lengthy consideration, the Court in an historic decision held that this prayer was a violation of the First Amendment and a breach of the principle of separation of church and state. The Court said in part:

There can be no doubt that New York's state prayer program officially establishes the religious beliefs embodied in the regents' prayer. The respondents' argument to the contrary, which is largely based upon the contention that the regents' prayer is "non-denominational" and the fact that the program, as modified and approved by state courts, does not require all pupils to recite the prayer but permits those who wish to do so to remain silent or to be excused from the room, ignores the essential nature of the program's constitutional defects. Neither the fact that the prayer may be denominationally neutral, nor the fact that its observance on the part of the students is voluntary can serve to free it from the limitations of the Establishment Clause. . . .

The Court concluded its opinion with these significant statements:

It is true that New York's establishment of its Regents' prayer as an officially approved religious doctrine of that State does not amount to a total establishment of one particular religious sect to the exclusion of all others—that, indeed, the governmental endorsement of that prayer seems relatively insignificant when compared to the governmental encroachments upon religion which were commonplace 200 years ago. To those who may subscribe to the view that because the Regents' official prayer is so brief and general there can be no danger to religious freedom in its governmental establishment, however, it may be appropriate to say in the words of James Madison, the author of the First Amendment: "[It] is proper to take alarm at the first experiment on our liberties. . . . Who does not see that the same authority which can establish Christianity, in exclusion of all other Religions, may establish, with the same ease any particular sect of Christians, in exclusion of all other Sects? That the same authority which can force a citizen to contribute three pence only of his property for the support of any one establishment, may force him to conform to any other establishment in all cases whatsoever?"

Finally, in June of 1963, the Supreme Court decided the two recent cases, *School District of Abington Township* v. *Schempp*[5] and *Murray* v. *Curlett*.[6]

In the *Schempp* case, the Schempp family brought a lawsuit to enjoin the enforcement of a Pennsylvania statute which required that at least ten verses from the Holy Bible should be read without comment at the opening of each public school on each school day. The statute further provided that any child should be excused from such Bible reading upon written request of his parent or guardian.

In the *Murray* case there was involved a rule of the Board of School Commissioners of Baltimore city, pursuant to authorizing provisions of the Maryland statutes, providing that the schools of the city hold opening exercises consisting primarily of the reading, without comment, of a chapter in the Bible and/or the use of the Lord's Prayer. The mother of a child attending the Baltimore schools brought the suit to require the Board to rescind and cancel this rule.

Ultimately, both of these cases reached the Supreme Court during its 1962-63 term and were argued and considered together. The Court handed down a single opinion, holding both the Pennsylvania statute and the Baltimore School Board rule to be unconstitutional. The majority opinion, written by Mr. Justice Clark, is comparatively brief. Justices Douglas, Brennan, Goldberg, and Harlan all wrote concurring opinions. Mr. Justice Stewart wrote a dissenting opinion. The majority opinion, the various concurring opinions, and the single dissenting opinion consume in all seventy pages of fine print, double column, large law book size in the lawyer's edition of the Supreme

Court Reports, and probably even more pages in the official reports printed under the direction of the Court. With this voluminous text, it is difficult to select one or two paragraphs and contend that they constitute the essence of the Court's decision. Indeed, in discussing this case lawyers and scholars find that the lengthy opinions and the different shades of reasoning, even among the eight of the nine Justices who concurred in the result, make it possible for almost anyone to find certain language which he feels tends to support his own preconceived notions of what the Court decided or should have decided.

The majority opinion incorporates certain language from the Court's earlier opinions referring to the concept that the government should be neutral on the question of religion and gives the concept of "neutrality" much greater emphasis than had been given in the earlier decisions. The Court pointed out that:

> The wholesome "neutrality" of which this Court's cases speak thus stems from a recognition of the teachings of history that powerful sects or groups might bring about a fusion of governmental and religious functions or a concert or dependency of one upon the other to the end that official support of the State or Federal Government would be placed behind the tenets of one or of all orthodoxies. This the Establishment Clause prohibits. And a further reason for neutrality is found in the Free Exercise Clause, which recognized the value of religious training, teaching and observance and, more particularly, the right of every person to freely choose his own course with reference thereto, free of any compulsion from the state. This the Free Exercise Clause guarantees. Thus, as we have seen, the two clauses may overlap. As we have indicated, the Establishment Clause has been directly considered by this Court eight times in the past score of years and, with only one Justice dissenting on the point, it has consistently held that the clause withdrew all legislative power respecting religious belief or the expression thereof. The test may be stated as fol-

lows: what are the purpose and the primary effect of the enactment? If either is the advancement or inhibition of religion then the enactment exceeds the scope of legislative power as circumscribed by the Constitution. That is to say that to withstand the strictures of the Establishment Clause there must be a secular legislative purpose and a primary effect that neither advances nor inhibits religion.

The Court then went on to say:

> Applying the Establishment Clause principles to the cases at bar we find that the States are requiring the selection and reading at the opening of the school day of verses from the Holy Bible and the recitation of the Lord's Prayer by the students in unison. These exercises are prescribed as part of the curricular school. They are held in the school buildings under the supervision and with the participation of teachers employed in those schools. . . . The trial court in No. 142 has found that such an opening exercise is a religious ceremony and was intended by the State to be so. We agree with the trial court's finding as to the religious character of the exercises.

Although this brings us up to date, it is not the end of the issue. The Supreme Court has not yet answered all of our questions, at least not to the extent that we can arrive at a complete unanimity of opinion on the role of religion in education. Undoubtedly further cases will be coming before the Court in the future, and the case of *Chamberlain* v. *The Dade County Board of Public Instruction*,[7] is in the Court already. The case, or more accurately the cases (there were two separate cases which were combined for trial and appeal), were filed by parents of certain school children in Dade County, Florida, challenging a broad range of practices that touch upon the question of religion in the public schools. Filed in 1960, long before the decision of the Supreme Court in the *Schempp* and *Murray* cases, this case referred to Bible reading, comment on the Bible, Bible distribution, Bible instruction after hours, the

Lord's Prayer, other prayers, grace, attitude during prayer, carols and hymns, Christmas and Easter observances, Hanukkah observances, religious symbols, baccalaureate services, religious census, and religious tests for selection or promotion of teachers —a veritable smorgasbord of issues.

There was a lengthy trial in the Circuit Court of Dade County in which evidence was introduced on all these matters. Following the trial, the Circuit Court entered an order early in 1961 which upheld the plaintiff's claim that the state and federal Constitutions were violated by sectarian comments on the Bible by public school teachers, use of school premises for after-hours Bible instruction, the exhibition of religious films, and the presentation of religious programs to observe Christmas, Easter, and Hanukkah. On the other hand, the Circuit Court found that no constitutional principles were violated by the Bible reading and prayer recitation. As to the holding of religious baccalaureate programs, the Circuit Court held that there was no evidence that they included "religious teachings." On the issue of a religious census in the schools, the Circuit Court held that there was no evidence that this was a regular practice. On the matter of religious tests for teachers, the Circuit Court held that this practice could not violate any right of the plaintiffs in their capacity as parents of school children.

With respect to those practices found unconstitutional by the Circuit Court, the school board did not take an appeal and presumably acquiesced in the lower court's decision. With respect to those portions of the court's order which held against the plaintiffs, an appeal was taken to the Supreme Court of Florida, which affirmed the decision of the Circuit Court. The plaintiffs appealed to the Supreme Court of the United States. This case was on file in the Court in June of 1963 at the time of the Court's decision in the *Schempp* and *Murray* cases, although it had not been argued before the Court. The Court took note of the case, but instead of deciding it, referred it back to the Supreme Court of Florida for reconsideration to determine whether that court might deem it necessary to modify some phases of its earlier decision in the light of the Supreme Court's decision in the *Schempp* and *Murray* cases.

The Supreme Court of Florida in January of 1964 reaffirmed its previous decision, stating in substance that it did not agree with the U.S. Supreme Court's decision in the *Schempp* and *Murray* cases and that the court did not wish to speculate on the interpretation of those or future Supreme Court decisions. Later the plaintiffs filed their case again in the Supreme Court of the United States, pointing out the action taken by the Florida Supreme Court and asking the Supreme Court of the United States to take jurisdiction and to decide the case.

One aspect of the overall situation which justifies mention is the proposal from various sources that there should be a Constitutional amendment on this subject. A proposed amendment has been introduced in the House of Representatives by Representative Becker of New York, which provides among other things that:

> Nothing in this Constitution shall be deemed to prohibit the offering, reading from, or listening to prayers or Biblical Scriptures, if participation therein is on a voluntary basis, in any governmental or public school, institution, or place.

Although the Becker amendment has been the most highly publicized, there have been many other proposed Constitutional amendments. Possibly more than one hundred different proposed amendments had been drafted. This entire matter may be in the hands of the Congress for some time, perhaps for generations.

In Summary

To try to summarize in capsule form the present state of the law is difficult. If I were to attempt to summarize in a few short sentences the essence of the legal principles laid down by the Supreme Court in these various decisions, it would be as follows: the state has a legitimate function in the education of its children. In carrying out this function through its public school system, it is fully entitled to delve into all phases of human knowledge and human history, including religion where religion constitutes an integral part of knowledge and history.

The state does not have a legitimate function in promoting religion, by virtue of the Establishment Clause of the First Amendment, nor in discouraging religion, by virtue of the Free Exercise Clause of the First Amendment. Therefore, the state, through its public school system, is not entitled to require or permit religious observances or any other act which has the effect of giving sponsorship or affirmative approval to a particular religion or to religion in general.

Chapter Four

•

HISTORICAL BACKGROUND

DAVID W. BEGGS, III

R. BRUCE McQUIGG

During the period when the American colonies were being settled, religious discussion was rife in England, the mother country, and throughout Europe. Calvinists were at odds with Methodists, while both were harassed by the Anglican majority, which included the English rulers. Baptists and Quakers disputed with Anglicans, Methodists, and Calvinists, while all Protestants were suspicious of Catholics. Refuge in the New World was sought by various European and English religious minorities who sought freedom to worship God in their own ways.

Though many settlers in the American colonies had crossed the ocean to avoid persecution or discrimination because of religious belief, few of them were willing to extend freedom of conscience to others. Thus many communities became bastions

David Beggs is a member of the faculty of the School of Education, Indiana University. Dr. Beggs has been both a teacher of history and a public school administrator. R. Bruce McQuigg is Associate Coordinator for Secondary Education, Project INSITE, Indiana University.

of one faith or another. In some colonies the Established Church of England prevailed, while in others dissenters found new and different establishments. The concept of establishment remained. Financial support was often given to a particular church through dedication of certain land for church use and allocation of a portion of the taxes raised in the colony; the church also solicited and received generous private donations from each family. Many colonies took firm positions favoring particular religious beliefs by punishing or even expelling nonbelievers.

In all the colonies except Delaware, New Jersey, Pennsylvania, and Rhode Island many civic privileges were confined to members of the established faith. The faith, though, varied from colony to colony. New England was the center of Puritanism, and Congregationalism was the orthodoxy of the Puritans. There were some settlements of Baptists, Presbyterians, and Quakers in New England, and even an occasional congregation of the Church of England, which later became the Episcopal Church. Although the Church of England was established in the southern colonies, they contained dissident groups of Baptists, Quakers, Huguenots, and Presbyterians. The central colonies were a mixture of faiths. Mennonites, Reformed Lutherans, Methodists, and some Catholics and Jews were to be found there along with Quakers, Presbyterians, Baptists, and Anglicans. All of these groups wanted to be free to worship as they chose.

During the seventeenth century the Puritans ruled their towns with stern religious zeal. Suffrage was given only to church members, and the congregation decided who might be a church member. Dissenters were dealt with harshly. Nevertheless, a good many individualists were to be found in New England. Roger Williams, expelled from Massachusetts for his advocacy of religious freedom, founded Rhode Island as a haven for everyone who wanted a choice to believe or not to believe as his conscience dictated. Williams' theory was that the foundation of government is popular sovereignty, not a divine plan, and that the church is only one of many social institutions. This theory, once a minority view, prevailed later when the Bill of Rights provided for separation of church and state.

Lord Baltimore established the colony of Maryland in 1634 as a refuge for Catholics. Other groups too were invited to Maryland. But by 1685 the era of tolerance was ended. Catholics lost not only religious freedom but also civil liberties. Open hostility broke out because of a widespread, unfounded rumor that the Catholics had made a pact with the Indians to kill all the Protestants. To many Protestants the suppression of the Catholics seemed the only guarantee of survival. Thus the hostility toward Catholics in Protestant America, which continued into the early twentieth century, was fed from anti-Catholic sentiments dating from an earlier period.

Educational Goals and Religion

It is instructive to contrast contemporary educational objectives and programs with those of the nation's early schools. Today's emphasis on a broad acquisition of knowledge, vocational skills, and the development of the individual child would have been entirely foreign to the American teacher in the eighteenth and early nineteenth centuries. Most Protestants believed that revelation through the Bible was the source of truth and salvation. Hence every child should be taught to read. To ensure that all children could do so, the colonists established public sectarian schools. Dissenters were not allowed to establish schools for their own children.

Puritans had an educated ministry. The ministers, forerunners of modern school superintendents, were the school's overseers—

selecting teachers, prescribing what should be taught, and dealing with parents who did not send their children to school. When it was not possible to employ a teacher, the minister frequently served in that capacity.

The clergy discussed the Bible in detail and required church members to know it intimately. Since Bible reading was essential for the practicing Protestant, education continued to be regarded as a necessary support of religion, except to the Quakers. Quakers held that any soul, regardless of the mind's ability, could communicate directly with the Holy Spirit. Thus education was not necessary for the religious exercises of this group, but Quakers did not oppose secondary schools and actually supported elementary schools.

Originally, the establishment of compulsory school attendance resulted largely from religious requirements. Later, in 1780, the Massachusetts Constitution provided:

> As the happiness of a people, and the good order and preservation of civil government, essentially depend on piety, religion, and morality; and as these cannot be generally diffused through a community but by the institution of public worship of God, and of public instructions in piety, their happiness, and to secure the good order and preservation of their government, the people of the commonwealth have a right to invest their legislature with power to authorize and require and the legislature shall, from time to time, authorize and require, the several towns, parishes, precincts, and other bodies politic, or religious societies, to make suitable provision at their own expense, for the institution of the public worship of God, and for the support and maintenance of public Protestant teachers of piety, religion, and morality, in all cases where such provision shall not be made voluntarily.
>
> And the people of this commonwealth have also a right to, and do, invest their legislature with the authority to enjoin upon all the subjects an attendance upon the instructions of the public teachers aforesaid, at stated time and seasons, if there be any on whose instructions they can conscientiously attend.[1]

The substance of education at the early levels was religious material. When not using the Bible, teachers relied on textbooks with a religious orientation. The *Hornbook*,[2] an early text, was predominantly made up of religious messages. Quakers and Mennonites used Pastorius' *New Primer*,[3] also based on Scripture. Those who did not speak English read the Bible and used related textbooks in their mother tongue.

While learning to read the catechism and the Bible was the central purpose of the colonial elementary school, grammar schools and academies, which had sprung up in the more populated areas, were primarily concerned with the preparation of ministers and lawyers. Usually attendance was limited to the sons and daughters of the upper classes. Boys who went through the secondary school were prepared for colleges; girls were prepared for their role in polite society. Although in these forerunners of today's high schools pupils were taught advanced subjects, the method of instruction consisted largely of exercises of rote memory.

Education in the New Nation

The establishment of American independence gave impetus to change and progress in many American institutions, including schools and churches. Many churches reorganized themselves on a national basis independent of the Old World churches from which they had sprung. The First Amendment to the Constitution guaranteed religious liberty and prohibited any established church. No doubt the adoption of the principle of separating church and state owed as much to the fact of religious pluralism and to preoccupation with the pressing problems encountered in the effort to build a new nation as to any lofty ideals of tolerance. In any case, in their new constitutions the states also adopted bills or rights guaranteeing religious toleration. One of the most famous state documents was Virginia's Statute of Religious Liberty (1785), the product of Jefferson, Madison, and Mason. Nevertheless Catholics and Jews were often still victims of prejudice and discrimination. The prevailing ethic in nineteenth-century America was Protestant—especially in the South—and this was evident in the character of the early public schools.

The nineteenth century saw the gradual adoption by all the states of the principle of universal, free, and compulsory education. Support from churches helped to make this ideal a reality. Its progress, however, was neither rapid nor unopposed. Under the Constitution responsibility for providing educational programs rested with the states. Hence diversity existed in both policies and practices in public education. Some states, mostly along the eastern coast, provided more and better education than did some states in the West, where community life was less stable and resources less adequate.

When schools could be formed during the westward expansion, they were modeled on those of the eastern seaboard states. However, less emphasis was given to the Bible and more attention was paid to mathematics and literature. No one church dominated the new communities, and books, teachers, and time for school were in short supply. Hence parents who wanted their children to get an education were in no position to insist on any particular theological auspices.

In the East, also, the wave of immigrants and the expansion of cities consequent on commercial growth diluted the once tight-knit communities. People sent their children to any school and, for the most part, were glad to get the available instruction. Material gain became more important in people's thinking; more emphasis was placed on prosperity and happiness in this world and less on the life to come. These tendencies were reflected in the gradual secularization of the school curriculum.

Yet religious influence in the schools lingered on. As late as 1963 ten states still required reading of the Bible in the schools.

A Change of Emphasis

Out of the social ferment over immigration in the period from 1830 to 1860 arose the great crusader for nonsectarian public education, Horace Mann, the head of the Massachusetts school system and the "father of public schools." Mann advocated divesting the curriculum of religious subjects. Although he saw education in terms of preparation for life on earth, he believed in the need for moral teaching. Rather than have the schools teach one religious view, he sought to have them inculcate moral principles such as truth, honesty, love, and justice. The Bible could be used as a reader, Mann said, but teachers should never make comments on it. Mann's views were influential but were not universally accepted.

During the nineteenth century an increasing number of Protestant denominations evolved, while at the same time enormous numbers of Catholics came to the United States from Europe. Fear of Catholic domination led in many places to renewed hostility toward Catholics. The Know Nothing party, established in 1853 by old-stock Americans, was alarmed by the Catholics flocking to the polls under the influence of political bosses. But because elections could be decided by a few thousand votes, politicians were not anxious to alienate any minority.

To Catholics religion was an integral part of the education of the young, and they did not wish to subject their children to any form of religious instruction other than their own. Hence Catholics founded schools at all levels—elementary, secondary, and collegiate—with the religious orders providing teachers. The expense was high, however, and some people felt that the existence of Catholic schools tended to accentuate social divisions in the community.

In a little over 150 years the nation's schools have developed from church-sponsored to state-sponsored institutions. Today schools exist to develop the whole man, not to perpetuate any one dogma. Yet the relationship of religion and education is still a thorny problem. Some notion of the controversies it has generated is given in Chapter Three on famous court decisions in this area.

A Door in the Wall

In the last few years there have been repeated attempts by educational groups to increase federal aid to education. Always the plea is for federal aid without federal control. Several kinds of bills have been put before the Congress. One group of bills called for financial aid from the federal government to all schools, public and private, for auxiliary services. Another group of bills, also unsuccessful, wanted federal aid for public schools only. Still a third group of defeated legislative proposals called for federal aid to be given to the states to be used as they saw fit and as their state constitutions provided.

In the years since World War II it has often been urged that the costs of providing the quality of education required in modern times cannot be financed by the property tax and other tax sources available to the states and local governments. But the role of the federal government in providing funds for public elementary and secondary schools has not been clearly delineated, partly because of the question of whether sectarian schools would get financial support. Whether or not the government, federal or state, should aid sectarian education was hotly debated at the time the Smith-Hughes Act was passed into law in 1917. This Act, aimed at furthering vocational and technical training, provided that no federal funds be used directly or indirectly for the support of any religious or privately owned school or college. This precedent has been cited over and over down to the 1965 Congress.

The Elementary and Secondary Education Act of 1965 has been heralded by some as a major breakthrough in the federal government's long history of attempts to support public education, and it has been criticized by others, who feel that it solves no problems. Three long-standing obstacles to federal aid (aid to parochial schools, racial segregation, and fear of federal control) were considered by those who drafted the Act.

The Act ensures that parochial schools shall receive some help, but the casual observer who may assume a complete breakdown of safeguards in this area should review the provisions of the Act more carefully. These provisions are arranged under five titles, under which the major portion of the proposed $1.25 billion yearly aid is to be distributed.

Title I is designed to provide special educational services to children in low-income families on a "population-per-area" basis. This title requires that educationally deprived children enrolled in nonpublic schools and residing in the school attendance area shall be served by the special educational programs funded under the title. Receiving specialized services "not normally provided" is a key phrase of this title. Such services are to be remedial, therapeutic, or pertaining to health and welfare. In fact, public school personnel may provide some of these services *in* the parochial school, provided the local educational agency and the state agency agree that distance, time, and numbers of children make such an arrangement feasible. Teachers in nonpublic schools cannot be paid from Title I funds but can participate in in-service programs and receive supervisory or advisory help made possible by the Act.

Another general provision is important to this relationship.

Classes conducted on public school premises as a part of a project may not be segregated on the basis of religious affiliation. Thus shared time, or dual enrollment, may become standard practice in communities which until now have never considered such a plan.

It is also clearly stated that the state educational agencies are to administer the funds of Titles I and II and that no payment of money is to be made to a nonpublic school within Title I.

Title II, which emphasizes school library resources, textbooks, and other instructional materials, is also intended to provide supplementary assistance to the student enrolled in a parochial school, and to his teachers—not directly to the school —by lending materials. It is estimated that fewer than one-half of all parochial school buildings have libraries. The involvement of these schools under Title II is likely to prove extensive.

Because of some state laws forbidding distribution of materials to nonpublic schools and because the Act intends the program to be administered within existing state laws, arrangements will have to be worked out differently in the various states. The United States Commissioner of Education is authorized to lend materials to those parochial schools faced by "insurmountable obstacles." The public agency in all cases will retain ownership of materials. Since the cost of such materials and administration of their distribution will be deducted from the state's allotment, it follows that few obstacles are likely to remain insurmountable.

Some observers say that educators in nonpublic schools are more enthusiastic about the "wide-open" Title III than about the others. Title III is concerned with supplementary educational services and provides for grants to local educational agencies. As Section 304(a) specifies, grants will be made "only if there is satisfactory assurance that in the planning of the program there has been, and in the carrying out of the program there will be, participation of the persons broadly representative of the cultural and educational resources of the area to be served." Nonpublic schools are specifically included in this broad representation and may apply for such grants. Further, provision must be made for children enrolled in nonpublic schools to participate in those services appropriate within grants made to public agencies.

Titles IV and V of the Act are not concerned with private and parochial schools in any new context, since they expand the existing cooperative research program and strengthen state educational agencies.

In summary, the Act intends to attack educational deprivation wherever it is found. Though it specifies participation of private and parochial school youngsters, distribution of materials to their libraries, and help for their teachers, it makes clear that direct aid (such as payment of salaries for private school teachers) shall not be made. Materials will not go directly from the Commissioner to a private school except in extreme cases. Many lawyers and administrators feel that the Act is a masterpiece of avoiding head-on the controversies over aid to nonpublic schools. *Time* magazine states that President Johnson "avoided the mistakes of his predecessors and produced an ingenious bill that neatly diffused the explosive issues."[4] Whether or not the Act will be successfully implemented remains to be seen.

Chapter Five

•

RELIGION IN THE SCHOOLS:
A PRESBYTERIAN'S VIEW

THERON B. MAXSON

One would be presumptuous to imagine that he could speak "for" Presbyterians on religion and education. However, it is generally recognized that Presbyterians would rally against any force which would seek to destroy or render ineffective the basic institutions of American education, particularly the public school system. In addition to their concern for the welfare of public elementary and secondary schools, Presbyterians have established many church-related colleges and for many decades have been in favor of higher education under state control. At

Dr. Maxson is the president of Hastings College, Hastings, Nebraska. He has been active in educational and Presbyterian Church groups, and has served as president of the Presbyterian College Union. He directed a study, with committee support, which led to the writing and presentation of the statement *The Church and the Public Schools*, prepared by the Board of Christian Education of the (then) Presbyterian Church in the United States of America, and approved as "An Official Statement" by the 169th General Assembly of that denomination in 1957. By intent and in many respects Dr. Maxson's discussion parallels or enlarges upon certain selected aspects of this "Statement."

this time Presbyterians are renewing their efforts in support of their church-related colleges, provided these schools are of quality and well oriented to their basic Christian purpose and capable of providing for a sound education.

The inherent "freedom to learn and know" within the Reformed tradition of Protestantism, which is clearly articulated throughout American Presbyterian history, has provided a major force underlying education at all levels. There are well-formulated reasons for this enthusiasm for the welfare of the free public school system. These reasons grow out of an interpretation of biblical theology, reaffirmed in basic form by the leaders of the Reformation, practiced with growing success since the American colonial days, and defended valiantly when threats have appeared.

The American public has demonstrated deep faith in education. It looks to the schools to define the nature and the shortcomings of the social and cultural structure. The public also expects the schools at all levels to provide high-quality educational experience in the expanding teaching areas of science, literature, government, fine arts, and related fields. Teaching responsibilities, traditionally a function of the home and sometimes of the church, have been placed more and more on the shoulders of the schoolteacher. The wide teaching-learning area known popularly as "moral and spiritual values" has in recent times been rather exclusively, and sometimes perhaps happily, relegated by some parents to the classroom. On the other hand, many parents view such values as derived from God and not primarily the outgrowths of human endeavor. Therefore they feel that these values are better kept within the province of the church and the home.

To the latter group education is incomplete without a theological base from which values emerge. While receiving possible encouragement from secular institutions, the implanting of these values rests specifically with the institutions uniquely prepared to teach them, namely the church and the family. Since the end of World War II the schools have been under unprecedented pressure to offer a vastly enlarged and more effective curriculum. Not only has the public placed greater emphasis upon good teaching, but also schools overwhelmed by postwar enrollments have found it necessary to reevaluate their total role within the culture. The problem of adequate guidance and counseling, drawn into focus as a result of growing juvenile delinquency and alleged general moral apathy, has sharpened the concern of thousands of conscientious parents, schoolmen, and churchmen to find better means of assisting students in developing a sound philosophy of life.

Reformed Theology and a Philosophy of Education

It is impossible to produce either a philosophy or a methodology in education that does not attempt to define the nature of man. For Presbyterians seeking a theological point of departure, the first step might well involve the theory of human personality drawn from a biblical interpretation of the nature of God.

Reformed theology, resorting to the Platonic system of logic, not only regards God as transcendent Sovereign Creator, but also reaffirms that God is known as a Person, not primarily through the natural order of life, but through the revelation of God in Jesus Christ. While the very orderliness of the universe defines in part the nature of the Fatherhood of God, His relationship to man standing in need of love, compassion, and redemption is conceived through Christ. Man is viewed as both incomplete and estranged from his full human heritage when apart from fellowship with God as revealed in Christ. The divine concern that man might achieve full fellowship with

God was evidenced by the sacrifice of God for mankind through the death and resurrection of Christ.

For the Presbyterian this gift of grace projects the nature of man and his potential into a unique perspective. It is as though the whole order of life, under God, conspired to draw humanity out of its egocentric, imperfect view of self, into a full inheritance, not the least expression of which is the right to be free to learn, to know, and to mature. This theological position makes man indeed only "a little lower than the angels." In simple language, no service or sacrifice, whether of divine origin or of human institution, should lie dormant if such disuse prevents man from reaching his appointed place as a member of God's family, capable of maximum growth and achievement in all capacities mental, physical, and spiritual. Man's measure of his own dignity, as conceived within a true democracy upholding the inherent right of a person to achieve opportunity for maturity, is in turn a by-product of God's redemptive love. Within this concept, the full freedom of the individual is advanced. Within this theological framework and carried out to its extreme implication, man is conceived to be unfettered in making his own decisions, including even the right to reject both God and his fellow humans. Judgments resting upon him by virtue of his choices are also his own to bear. This suggests much as to the nature of education.

Calvinistic theology places man at the heart of a sacred trust. Man's task is to preserve, develop, and cultivate the world as a means of glorifying God. There is yet another dimension. To John Calvin, society itself was an order of creation: society consisted of both the "redeemed" and the "unredeemed." Both could profit from education. This theologian, so important to Presbyterians, did not conceive "the elect of God" as perfect or sinless, but as those who need a proper environment to achieve full and orderly growth. Persons who have made no Christian confession also need education to inform themselves in order to participate with others in the process of building a good social structure. Education was a prime tool. Calvin's respect for civil government in Geneva was an example of his philosophy at work. The Christian has the responsibility, under God, to achieve sufficient knowledge to impose upon himself law and order. A theory of universal education, providing studies for both the Christian and the non-Christian, is apparent in Calvin's thought.

The leaders of the Reformation were well aware that ignorance and illiteracy in the masses would never provide the milieu within which the Kingdom of God on earth could take root. Within the social institutions of government, church, and home, this idealism provided a whole new appraisal of the task of schooling children and youth. The early Protestant church fathers saw a growing affinity between religious teaching and secular knowledge. Clerical and secular leaders since have experienced a new era of give and take, affecting civil government and a broadened school curriculum. The "Enlightenment" saw the increased importance of the lay teacher to such developing academic areas as science, art, and literature, and especially religious teaching.

While the curriculum has enlarged considerably since the sixteenth century, from reading the Scriptures in the monastery school to studying nuclear physics in a classroom filled with children of pluralistic religious persuasions, Presbyterians have become increasingly convinced that the freedom to learn and make decisions is one of God's supreme gifts to men. Universal educational opportunity is in part an outgrowth of a deep and growing confidence in man's potential as a learner. The right of all to be educated has emerged as a sacred obligation.

Another theological tenet is relevant to the problem of methodology in education. Presbyterians have adhered closely to the doctrine sometimes called "The Priesthood of all Believers." Man in a sense provides his own sacerdotal direction; he takes his petitions and contritions to God in private confessional; he may be led through varying religious and cultural experiences into positions of belief somewhat at variance with those of other Christians. The very freedom he enjoys in his approach to God and in his search for truth is an element most compatible to the Reformed theology of Presbyterianism. In addition to this direct personal communication with God, all persons within the Christian community are called on to perform a unique function as members of the communion and as members of society. The layman and the clergyman alike are called to a specific task. All men have a distinct contribution to make to other men, serving as Christians and priests. This concept of the individual as inclusive is regarded as not only monumental but also imperative to the development of the freedoms that men are privileged to enjoy as they participate in the building of social institutions.

Religion for Presbyterians Not Expressed Through Isolation

Presbyterians have never been much inclined to conceive worship and true piety in isolation from the mainstream of social living. While the Presbyterian Church has defended the right of other religious groups to establish orders and educational institutions of a cloistered or ecclesiastical nature for the chief purpose of propagating a specific doctrinal position, the Presbyterian-related elementary and secondary schools for the most part have never succeeded in establishing themselves for

long. At the time of the Civil War many Presbyterian grammar schools were established or supported by congregations.
These efforts were short-lived, since apparently most Presbyterians were convinced of the necessity of joining others of
the community, even those of different religious beliefs, in supporting some type of community school effort, except in "home
mission areas." Efforts to revive the grammar schools have
been made throughout the century since that time, but such
movements almost always fail. Most Presbyterians have demonstrated their desire that their children be a part of the community school, where children reared in varying theological
positions and divergent social opportunity learn together.

Before the establishment of a solid system of secondary
schools under public support, the academy, under church direction, was common in many denominations. While certainly
linked with an effort to provide religious values and knowledge,
the academy was for the most part the result of a frontier attempt to provide education beyond the elementary level. A
number of academies were associated with or later became
church-related colleges. Again Presbyterians demonstrated their
enthusiasm to provide community education for all children
and demonstrated their confidence by enrolling their own
children in public schools.

> We have always acknowledged a Christian responsibility to the
> whole community about us, even to those who do not share
> our faith. As for the actual situation, we have found it possible
> in the religiously mixed society of America to participate
> actively in institutions such as the government and the public
> schools, because their necessary religious impartiality generally
> leaves adequate room for the development and expression of
> Christian commitment. The public schools in particular are
> shaped by the deliberate effort to respect the integrity of every
> child and to encourage the widest freedom and discussion in

the child's search for truth. Having this character, they are an unrivaled agency for meeting the needs of all our people individually and our national society as a whole.[1]

School Climate and Curriculum

The place of religion and spiritual values in the curriculum of public school children has been the topic of many educational conferences at a time in which overwhelming numbers of school children and youth have crowded into classrooms. Instructors are keenly aware that the whole order of human existence is under scrutiny and reevaluation by the students. Pupils and teachers are often driven to find moral and spiritual implications underlying community living. As never before they are examining national and cultural movements which are no longer capable of existing in monolithic isolation. The drive of young nations demanding autonomy, the magnitude of new scientific knowledge and skill requiring direction, the deepening understanding of the civil rights issue—all of these are social and scientific revolutions that can no longer be studied as something apart from the curriculum. A knowledge of peoples and cultures, including the interplay between culture and religion, can no longer be avoided. Within this framework it is difficult to conceive of a classroom of any type, seriously engaged in intensive examination of the culture and heritage of the race, without understanding the role of religion in human experience. Knowledge of the place of religion in life is necessary to a thorough education, and it is difficult for many to imagine a sturdy value system without religion. American history is full of examples of the commitment of people to religious faith, which has motivated them to establish a variety of institutions for social betterment.[2]

Institutional religion and personal religious belief, which in the past have led to commitment, are also being reexamined and questioned by a dynamic student world. There is evidence that this is true not only in the colleges but also in the elementary and high schools. American students are not necessarily anxious to reject religious faith or practice, but they are keenly anxious to know of their verities. The close proximity of death to life, brought into focus by the threats of nuclear warfare, has provided heavy psychological overtones in the life of the contemporary pupil. The student cannot escape self-examination within the very complexity of political and international conflict. Daily he is forced to accept or reject moral responsibilities within his own interpersonal relationships. Reference to moral and spiritual values are inescapable within the classroom, and sooner or later discussions lead into such depth that they become involved in a distinctly religious dimension. Religious sanctions, religious literature, religious practices and the role of denominations or faiths are all brought consciously or unconsciously into the academic arena.

A classroom climate which meets the student's quest for understanding the place of religion can embody religious content and favorable teaching attitudes without violation of our fundamental principle of separation of church and state. Public tax-supported education should under no condition be allowed to indoctrinate in any specific religious belief. Sectarianism is out of order in the public school classroom. Individual conscience and constitutional guarantees must be reckoned with. This need not eliminate a climate which would encourage a child to explore in depth the meaning and values of his own religious faith, but the public schools are not institutions of religion. While the school can and should provide encouragement and information supporting the student's quest for religious knowledge and commitment, individualized faith must depend ultimately upon extra-public-school institutions, chiefly the home and the church or synagogue. In turn, the schools, committed to the principle of free exercise of research and study, should provide full opportunity through carefully devised teaching procedures for the student to know of the religious heritage of our people. The classroom, whether public or private, cannot voluntarily divorce itself from discussion about the place of religion and religious groups in our national life. Excursions into the humanities can scarcely be complete or fully respect the wide search for truth without an encounter with religion.

The educator, well versed in educational psychology, knows that knowledge alone does not necessarily produce appreciations or attitudes congenial to the building of any value system. Values and judgments seldom become meaningful or personalized apart from feelings generated, often unconsciously, within teaching media. Instructional attitudes represent a basic consideration in the whole matter of the teaching of moral and spiritual values, particularly those related to religion.

Unfortunately the average school teacher has been given little guidance in his task of correlating the curricular, psychological and legal phases of the place of religion in education. Much more attention should be given by teacher training institutions to assist teachers to reinterpret the meanings, including those of a religious nature, which have influenced our national life. Educational workshops, experimentation, and more intensive training can provide teachers with a deeper understanding of the place of religion within regular curricular materials and of how appreciations and values can be added to more intellectualized studies without violation of individual conscience. While indoctrination in specific religious beliefs is out of order, the respect for an individual position on religion as derived from any particular church or home is equally fundamental to the inherent right of a student in his free search for truth. The climate of a school should sustain any and all students in their beliefs about religion. Give and take on religious topics does indeed take place in the American classroom. This appears to be healthy since few teachers seem to abuse the principle of academic freedom to favor any sectarian position.

A general climate supporting the child in his search for religious truth may be of as much or more worth to the child than formal courses or exercises in religion. Regular school subjects offer a wide opportunity for investigation and appreciation of the place of religion in music, art, literature and the like. Textbooks should refer with academic integrity to the contributions of the great ethnic faiths as they have influenced subject areas. Teaching impartially about religion and with true respect for the religious quest of the race adds a firm dimension consistent with the heritage of our American educational system.

If this seems to be a pragmatic approach supporting the natural place of religion in the public school classroom, it should also point to a danger threatening inherent freedoms. States rightly require school attendance in the early years of life. Most parents by choice or through financial restrictions choose for their children a public education over the private or parochial school. Catholics, Protestants, Jews and many sects are thus receiving instruction simultaneously under a teacher who in turn may be a committed member in any one of a large number of religious denominations or faiths. Wide experimentation within certain states has made provision for courses in Biblical material for public school students. Such instruction is offered on a voluntary basis. Released-time programs have been instituted in many states with varying results. More recently a shared-time program is being studied and at points is under trial. Without doubt many innovations, correlations, and improvements on any of these plans will receive more attention during the next decade. Careful experimentation is essential.

The position which has been stated thus far need not imply that religious neutrality, even when it supports the student's quest for his own religious commitment, should be the only approach offered the child. It simply implies that the public schools were neither erected nor empowered to fulfill the specific functions of a church or of the home in providing religious instruction in doctrine or sectarian belief. Conversely, the church and the home are under an ever-increasing pressure to provide a complete and clearly articulated instruction in doctrine and ecclesiastical faith climaxed through worship. Presbyterians find it difficult, if not impossible, to formulate a full-scale value system purely on any humanistic scale or through any secular institution, since God is Lord of all of life and the prime source of all value and truth.

> We must never betray the genius of the public schools, nor yet be mesmerized by the fatal assumption that the church can delegate its responsibility to any institution in order to make up for the prevalence of religious illiteracy. We hold that the home, the church, and the synagogue must share fully in processes of refining and supporting the general attempts of the school in recognizing the value of religious attitudes as applied to its regular school subjects and in its other areas of nurturing child growth.

> We believe that a "common core" or residuum of religious belief agreeable to all faiths as a basis for teaching is insufficient and misleading; that religious commitment arises in a specific and concrete religious community, highly articulate, and never abstracted into common elements. As Presbyterians we believe that human relationships derive their meanings from God as known through Jesus Christ and nurtured through the sacraments and through teaching within the fellowship of the church. Although other denominations may hold belief in

a core of faith that is different, most, even within that difference, hold to a faith in a transcendent God to whom we owe
our highest allegiance. The highly specific beliefs and convictions derived from this central position are incompatible with
a "faith of synthesis." While we neither expect nor desire any
teacher to indoctrinate any form of sectarianism, neither do
we countenance the teaching of devitalized "common faith" as
a proper substitute for highly specific religious belief. We encourage the schools, therefore, in emphasizing the religious
heritage of students, but we reject the assumption that such
an emphasis can be the answer to our quest for adequate religious education for our youth.[3]

The Reformed tradition of religion, therefore, conceives all
truth as of divine source and encourages all persons to search
for truth. Ecclesiastical and secular groups participate alike in
the educative task. These tenets are not incompatible with a
developing theory of modern education. Educational psychology and educational sociology have added insight into the
nature of the child within his group. Many types of teachers
and many social institutions present a variety of "live options"
to the maturing student. Parents and church-oriented teachers
share with many other educators in the community to make
optimum provision for growth of every child. This has meant
a partial shift away from educational practices as controlled by
the church.

The home can never relegate its share of the teaching function to any institution. It must assume an ever-enlarging part of
religious education. There are still grave questions as to whether
or not parents have accepted this responsibility even though
specific and highly personalized beliefs belong to the family and
to the church. The act of worship, a distinct sacerdotal function, is fundamental to the development of a religious dimension for dedicated living and must always remain within the

right of the church supported by the home. Full commitment to the nature and purposes of God, as derived through worship and doctrinal studies, should never expect more than general motivation and encouragement by the public schools.

Financial Support for Schools

Expanding costs and increasing drain on the tax dollar for elementary and secondary education are a prime topic in most American communities. Heavy building programs resulting from vastly enlarged enrollments or outdated plants, expanded curricula calculated to meet the increasing demands set in motion by a new scientific-technological era, and competition for skilled educators represent some of the reasons for rising costs. School budgets have enlarged accordingly.

Both public and parochial schools have experienced the heavy burden of meeting fiscal obligations. While upholding the right of a religious body to maintain parochial schools, Presbyterians have resisted vigorously efforts to throw the public tax dollar into the support of parochial schools. Arguments, many and varied, usually cluster about two principles. In the first place, parochial elementary and secondary schools are under the governance of a church or denomination and exist as sectarian institutions. To use public tax funds for support of these schools, not under public control, however good their educational ability may be, might well in effect constitute a form of establishment of religion by government. In the second place, there is a very practical consideration. The further division of available public funds for schools could well impair the effectiveness of the public schools. Grave dangers to the body politic are inherent within any attempt to provide public tax support for parochial education. Just as the public school must be protected from sectarianism by constitutional guarantee, the free exercise of religion in all of its forms must be protected from public control. Both the church and the state must weigh with great care the implications and risks involved within the full dimensions of this problem.

Chapter Six

•

A LUTHERAN LOOKS AT
RELIGION AND EDUCATION

ARTHUR L. MILLER

The Lutheran point of view on the role of church and state in education might well take cues from the expression "God's right and left hands," used by Luther to symbolize the church and the state. This point of view emphasizes that both the church and the state have been established by God for the welfare of the human family.[1]

The church—God's right hand—is the instrument of God to carry out the twin responsibilities of missionary outreach and Christian education made explicit by Jesus in the great commission: "Go therefore and make disciples of all nations, baptizing them in the name of the Father, and of the Son, and of the Holy Spirit, teaching them to observe all that I have commanded you. . . ."[2] Education is of vital importance to the church, for Chris-

Dr. Miller is the Executive Secretary of Parish Education, Lutheran Church-Missouri Synod in St. Louis, Missouri. He has participated in three White House Conferences on Children, Youth, and Education and has written widely in church publications.

tian education is an organized and systematic program designed to help the members of the Body of Christ grow spiritually.

The state—God's left hand—is the instrument of God to keep law and order, to serve God's purposes, and to help advance the welfare of mankind. Every state requires a central conformity in beliefs, loyalties, and practice in order to maintain cultural and social organization. This means that the education of youth is a matter of vital importance in every state. Compulsory education laws seek to ensure for every citizen a good education that will equip him for discharging the duties of citizenship.

Education as a Shared Responsibility

The home, the church, and the state have deep concerns in education. At times these concerns result in parallel programs of activity; at other times there must be accommodations to adjust the separate roles to avoid conflict of interest.

From the Christian point of view, the home is the basic agency of Christian education. Indeed, the Christian home can be thought of as a Christian school with the parents serving as Christian teachers to develop Christian understandings, customs, and values. This role of the home in Christian education is emphasized by: "Fathers, do not provoke your children to anger, but bring them up in the discipline and instruction of the Lord."[3]

The church cooperates with the home by setting up various educational agencies. Since God does not designate the agencies of Christian education that a congregation is to establish, the congregation is free to choose the program that best serves the needs of its members. Some congregations leave the matter of general education to the public school and are satisfied with a program of Christian education that supplements the education offered in public schools. Other congregations desire an integration of religious education with general education and therefore sponsor church-related elementary schools and high schools.

The interest of the state in education is based on its concern that each generation of youth be prepared to discharge the duties of citizenship in time of peace and in time of war. The Court of Appeals in Kentucky stated it this way in *City of Louisville* v. *Commonwealth:* "Upon preparation of the younger generations for civic duties depends the perpetuity of this government."[4] The function of the public school is not to confer benefits upon the individual, even though this does happen; rather, the school exists because the very existence of civil society demands it. The compulsory education laws of the states emphasize that all children are to be educated. While most children attend the public school, the state recognizes that attendance at nonpublic schools also satisfies the compulsory attendance laws. Such nonpublic schools, including church-related schools, must meet substantially the same standards as the state requires of its own schools.

Christian Education as a Supplement to Secular General Education

In the early Christian Church, instruction was given individually by parents, deacons, and other members of the church. Later, catechumen schools were opened with courses of instruction lasting over several years. Instruction in secular subjects was received from parents, private tutors, and heathen schools. Christian education was stimulated as a result of the Reformation. Luther advocated universal education. While urging the state to carry on and enforce a program of general education, Luther's emphasis was on Christian education. He said, "Where the Holy Scriptures do not rule, I certainly advise no one to send his child."

The early public schools in the United States were markedly influenced by the religious leaders of the communities in which they were established. With the rise of the secular public school the church was faced with a momentous option: Should the church favor general education under secular auspices for members of the church, or should the church provide general education under Christian auspices? Some church groups and congregations have tried to develop a satisfactory program of Christian education on Sundays and weekdays outside of regular school hours.

The Sunday school is the most widely used of the church schools. When the Sunday school is staffed with trained teachers, when adequate lesson materials are provided, when administration and supervision are provided, and when facilities and equipment are adequate, the Sunday school can provide sound Christian education.[5] Even under ideal conditions, however, the Sunday school lacks sufficient time to provide a comprehensive program of Christian education. For this reason many congregations have provided additional time through vacation Bible schools and a variety of weekday schools.

Weekday schools include three types: *Released time,* with religious instruction during the time the children are released by the public school to the local church; *Midweek school,* with religious instruction for one to three hours after school; and *Saturday school,* with religious instruction for two to three hours on Saturday morning or afternoon. Each one of these programs requires trained teachers, suitable lesson materials, and adequate facilities if an effective educational experience is to be provided.[6]

The vacation Bible school, conducted for two or three hours

per day for two or three weeks in the summer, provides a depth experience in Christian education for many children. Again, the same requirements of trained teachers, suitable lesson materials, and adequate facilities are needed to make the vacation Bible school an effective educational experience.

Christian Education in Church-Related Elementary and Secondary Schools

The nonpublic schools of our country include many church-related schools. These schools are important educational resources of the nation. The following statement from *The State and Non-Public Schools,* by Fred F. Beach and Robert F. Will of the United States Office of Education, points up the place of nonpublic schools in our nation:

> Non-public educational institutions are and always have been a significant part of the Nation's total educational resources. These institutions serve millions of American youth and adults each year. They play an enormous role in transmitting our cultural heritage and enriching it. They make contributions at all levels of education and in all areas. They exert a tremendous influence in fashioning the American way of life.[7]

According to recent statistics approximately fourteen per cent of the pupils in the United States at the elementary and secondary level are in nonpublic schools. The vast majority of these are church-sponsored schools. Table I shows the church-related elementary school enrollment for the year 1965-1966. Table II shows the church-related secondary enrollment for the same year.

Since there are comparatively few church groups that maintain their own schools, it is difficult for many persons to understand why any church body should maintain such schools. Without attempting to speak for other groups that maintain

TABLE I. CHURCH-RELATED ELEMENTARY SCHOOLS
(K through grade 8)
1965-1966
Protestant Schools

Lutheran Synods	Year	Schools	Teachers	Enrollment
The Lutheran Church-Missouri Synod	1965	1,374	6,236	161,357
Wisconsin Evangelical Lutheran Synod	1965	228	893	24,810
American Lutheran Church	1965	56	251	6,281*
Lutheran Church in America	1963	16	89	1,830
Evangelical Lutheran Synod	1965	11	13	264
Synod of Evangelical Lutheran Churches	1963	2	7	188
Church of the Lutheran Confession	1965	8	18	424
Total		1,695	7,507	195,154

Other Protestant Denominations	Year	Schools	Teachers	Enrollment
Los Angeles Baptist City Mission Society	1965	25	190	4,246
Mennonite Christian Day Schools	1965	247	397	10,271
National Association of Christian Schools	1965	230	2,171	32,000
National Union of Christian Schools	1965	239	1,790	48,369
Protestant Episcopal Church	1965	228	Est. 1,000	26,378**

TABLE I. *(Continued)*

Other Protestant Denominations	Year	Schools	Teachers	Enrollment
General Conference of Seventh-Day Adventists	1965	1,014	2,792	45,855
Southern Baptist Convention	1964	44	—	Often lower grades only
General Council of the Assemblies of God	1965	20	133	2,386***
Religious Society of Friends	1963	44	—	6,158****
Total		2,091***	8,473***	175,663***

Other Church-Related Schools

Religious Group	Year	Schools	Teachers	Enrollment
Roman Catholic	1963	10,775	115,468	4,546,360
Hebrew	1965	233	—	52,300

*80 additional congregations of the American Lutheran Church maintain separate kindergartens with 2,689 enrolled.

**285 additional separate kindergartens and nursery schools with 9,600 enrolled.

***8 separate kindergartens with 374 enrolled.

****1,740 in preschool.

*****Some Protestant denominational or private interdenominational schools are not included in the figures because they are not affiliated with any group that compiles the statistics.

Note: Not all groups compile statistics on the number of teachers. For this reason this number has in some cases been estimated.

Public School Statistics, 1965-1966 Estimate: 81,910 schools; 971,000 teachers, 30,500,000 enrollment.

Board of Parish Education
The Lutheran Church-Missouri Synod
12-28-65

TABLE II. CHURCH-RELATED SECONDARY SCHOOLS (Grades 9-12)

1965-1966

Protestant Church-Related Secondary Schools

Lutheran Community High Schools	Year	Schools	Teachers	Enrollment
The Lutheran Church-Missouri Synod	1965	24*	583	11,179
Wisconsin Evangelical Lutheran Synod	1965	8*	136	2,565
Church of the Lutheran Confession	1965	1	2	36
Totals		32*	721	13,780

*One school is maintained jointly by the Missouri and Wisconsin Synods for a net total of 32 schools. The school is credited to each group except in the net total of 32 schools. Each group is credited with its share of the enrollment.

High Schools, Other Protestant Denominations	Year	Schools	Teachers	Enrollment
National Union of Christian Schools	1965	35	530	8,325
National Association of Christian Schools	1965	50	225	6,656
General Conference of Seventh-Day Adventists	1965	265	749	7,919
Mennonite	1965	8	90	1,214
Protestant Episcopal Church	1965	15	Est. 300	5,416
Los Angeles Baptist City Mission Society	1965	1	18	239
General Council of the Assemblies of God	1965	2	14	200
Religious Society of Friends	1963	27	Est. 300	5,911
Totals		403	Est. 2,226	35,880

TABLE II. *(Continued)*

Lutheran Boarding High Schools Connected with Colleges that Train for Church Vocations	Year	Schools	Teachers	Enrollment
The Lutheran Church-Missouri Synod	1965	11	—	1,397
Wisconsin Evangelical Lutheran Synod	1965	4	60	898
Church of the Lutheran Confession	1965	1	8	56
Evangelical Lutheran Synod	1965	1	5	7
Totals		17	—	2,358

Protestant Boarding Academies	Year	Schools	Teachers	Enrollment
American Lutheran Church	1965	3	36	490
Evangelical Lutheran Synod	1965	1	6	52
Protestant Episcopal Church	1965	103	Est. 1,250	25,092
General Conference of Seventh-Day Adventists	1965	46	1,097	9,828
Southern Baptist Convention	1962	12	237	3,479
National Association of Christian Schools	1965	6	90	2,200
Mennonite	1965	3	62	890
General Council of the Assemblies of God	1965	2	26	250
Totals		176	Est. 2,804	42,281

Other Church Related Schools

Group Maintaining Schools	Year	Schools	Teachers	Enrollment
Roman Catholic	1963	2,430	51,038	1,044,446
Hebrew	1965	90	—	11,500

Public School Statistics, 1965-1966 Estimate: 25,350 schools; 720,000 teachers; 11,500,000 enrollment.

Board of Parish Education
The Lutheran Church-Missouri Synod
12-28-65

full-time Christian elementary and high schools, the position of
the Lutheran Church-Missouri Synod provides an illustration of
the motivation behind the establishment of such schools.

Each Lutheran elementary school or high school is established, maintained, and controlled by the local congregation or
by a group of congregations. The decision to found a school,
the initiative that supplies the planning of program and facilities, and the leadership that keeps the membership interested in
the school and willing to support it comes from the local
congregation.

What moves a congregation to establish and maintain a
school or to cooperate in establishing an interparish Lutheran
elementary school or a Lutheran high school? Generally a deep
concern for the spiritual well-being of the children and youth
of the church initiates such action. More specifically, congregations are prompted by reasons like these:

1. The Christian school makes it possible to teach the Word of
   God thoroughly.
2. The Christian school makes it possible to apply the Word of
   God to all school subjects and, like the Christian home, im-
   parts Christian instruction throughout the day.
3. The Christian school assists the home in providing Christian
   training. It seeks to foster Christian attitudes and Christian
   behavior.
4. The Christian school provides Christian fellowship. Children benefit from their association with Christian teachers
   and pupils.
5. The Christian school provides adequate time for Christian
   education. The achievement of the objectives of such education is a slow process, as is the achievement of any worthwhile goal. Regular daily instruction in God's Word, plus
   the opportunity to correlate religious instruction with
   music, art, and other school subjects provides more time for

Christian education than any other agency or combination of agencies.

6. The Christian school uses professional teachers who bring to the teaching of God's Word the same professional skill that teachers generally bring to the teaching of the regular school subjects.

Many congregations find these compelling reasons for providing the opportunity for Christian education at its best, in a church-sponsored school.

Similarities and Differences Between Church-Sponsored Schools and Public Schools

When the church engages in general education, the outward arrangements and methods used do not differ markedly from those of public education. Teachers in Christian schools apply the insights of child development and educational method in much the same way as teachers in public schools. Also, the subject matter studied at the several grade levels is much the same, except for the addition of the subject of religion.

The difference between the Christian school and the public school are in the respective total philosophies of the schools, which operate on different assumptions, aim at different objectives, and operate with different conceptions of knowledge.

The assumptions of the school program, those which teachers take for granted, are numerous. These assumptions are related to the nature of the universe, the nature of man, the nature of truth, and the goal of education. Five beliefs undergird teaching in the Lutheran school.

1. The Lutheran school emphasizes that this is God's world, created by Him.
2. The Lutheran school emphasizes that man is God's creation;

that man has a body and soul; that man is sinful by nature; that God wants men to be saved; that through faith in Christ man receives forgiveness of sin, eternal life, and salvation, and again becomes a child of God.

3. The Lutheran school recognizes several sources of truth. The Holy Scriptures are God's truth for man in spiritual matters; reason, science, and experience are additional sources of truth.

4. The Lutheran school sees the goal of education as the perfecting of saints who are equipped to function as kings and priests of God.

5. The Lutheran school recognizes the validity of the objectives of general education such as the four major groups of objectives developed by the Educational Policies Commission: self-realization, human relationship, economic efficiency, and civic responsibility.

While the Lutheran school must include these concerns in its program, it goes beyond them to such additional foundational objectives as these: (1) an understanding of the nature of the true God and man's relationship to Him; (2) a growing Christian character; (3) the love of fellow man through application of Christian principles in all relationships; (4) a rich devotional life as a source of spiritual strength; (5) an active participation in the life and work of the church; (6) the dedication of time, talents, and treasures to God in a life of faithful stewardship.

The basic difference between the objectives of the public school and the church-sponsored school is this: The objectives of the public school necessarily relate to man in his relationships with individuals, groups, and institutions in his society, while the goals of the Christian school relate to these relationships plus man's relationship to God. Indeed, the Christian school emphasizes that man's relation to God is the source of guidance to man in his concept of self and in his relationships with individuals, groups, and institutions.

Attitude Toward Public Education of Those Who Sponsor Church-Related Schools

The right of parents to send their children to nonpublic schools and the right of private groups to establish schools, including church-sponsored schools, is a matter of settled constitutional law. In spite of these facts, there have been numerous attacks on church-sponsored schools by certain individuals and groups. Some of these attacks arise out of a difference in theological positions; some of them arise out of a zeal for public education which sees the church-related school as detracting from good public schools; some of them arise out of the totalitarian view that the welfare of the nation requires a governmental monopoly in education.

With respect to difference in theological position, some church denominations believe that there must be complete freedom of inquiry also in the area of religion. The Lutheran Church-Missouri Synod believes that Christian education must be transmissive, for the Great Commission recorded in Matthew 28:19-20 sets a teaching task for the church that requires the teaching of the truths of God.

With respect to the charge that church-sponsored schools weaken the public schools by drawing away the educational interest of many citizens from the public schools, it is a fact that this need not happen and does not actually occur in many communities. The Lutheran Church-Missouri Synod agrees that the public schools should be a matter of concern to all American citizens. The Synod has repeatedly emphasized that the development of its elementary schools and high schools is not to be interpreted as a criticism of public schools, disinterest in them, or unwillingness to support them. The Synod urges its members to take an interest in the public schools and to support them.

With respect to the view that church-related schools accentuate differences and create a division in the community, it is true that the church-sponsored schools separate a segment of the population from the public schools. But whether or not this encourages an undesirable separateness is another matter. It is a strange contention that only a monopolistic educational program will develop common understanding and trust among the members of the community as fellow citizens. Democracy is hospitable to cultural pluralism and strong enough to allow diversity and forsake a monopoly in education. Children and youth attending church-sponsored schools are trained for loyal, active, and intelligent Christian citizenship. Congregations that maintain Christian schools believe that the development of such Christian citizenship makes a definite contribution to the strength of the nation.

Every denomination, every congregation, and every parent must decide how God's requirements for Christian education can best be met. Every effort at Christian education is worthwhile in contributing to spiritual growth. From many points of view the Lutheran Church-Missouri Synod believes that the church-sponsored school is Christian education at its best. Not all pupils can attend such a school. Indeed, some congregations cannot develop or may not want such a school. However, the church-sponsored school remains a live option for many parents, and pupils who attend such a school receive a more comprehensive Christian education than that provided by other agencies.

Religion in the Public School Program

As American education passed from private to public sponsorship and control, a definite attempt was made to avoid the teaching of sectarian religion in the public schools. The gradual elimination of religion from education in the elementary schools of our nation was a development in our history which was necessary for the preservation of religious liberty.

In recent years public school and church leaders have made a large-scale exploration of the problem of religion in the public school. Two major reports were issued by public school educators: *Moral and Spiritual Values in the Public Schools* issued by the Educational Policies Commission of the National Education Association and the American Association of School Administrators;[8] and *The Relation of Religion to Public Education* issued by the American Council on Education.[9] A significant contribution to this discussion, made by the study document prepared by the Committee on Religion and Public Education of the National Council of the Churches of Christ in the U.S.A., was entitled *Relation of Religion to Public Education.*[10]

The Lutheran Board of Parish Education included in its report to the Synodical Convention in 1953 the following statement on religion in the public schools:

It is clear that there are some things that the public schools cannot do so far as the teaching of religion is concerned. They cannot teach the doctrine of a denominational religion. They cannot teach a "common core" of religious and ethical ideas that goes beyond acknowledgment of the existence of God and man's obligation to the Moral Law.

The public school can, however, take a positive attitude toward religion and toward moral and spiritual values. This positive attitude requires, first, including moral and spiritual values in the statement of aims of the school. Such aims should be developed by the teaching staff and should involve the participation, the interest, and the concern of the general public. Second, the public school should avoid opposing and ridiculing religious beliefs. As Christians, we emphatically assert that such opposition is as much a denial of religious liberty as advocating a religious belief in the classroom. Third, the public school can teach about religion. It can point to the large role that religion plays in the lives of many people. It can point to the influence religion has on the conduct of many people. It can point to the influence religion has exerted upon society in maintaining morality. It can very properly study religious art and religious music and make use of such materials in the school program. It can provide for Bible reading without comment in the regular school program. Such factual study of religion does not commit the public school to a particular religious belief. Fourth, the public school can evidence respect for the several religious faiths and observances in the community. This respect should also extend to the rights of those who are irreligious to hold their opinions. The public school has no right, however, to subtly advocate atheism by a blanket of silence around everything that concerns religion or religious faith and life.[11]

Bible Reading and Prayer in the Public Schools

There has been a variety of practices in the states concerning Bible reading and prayer in the public schools. The problem of praying by a group of pupils representing various faiths has agitated some individuals and groups for many years. Since prayer constitutes an act of worship, many believed that it had no place at all in the public school classroom or assembly. Reactions to the Supreme Court decisions on the religion-education issue are varied. Some persons are very upset because, despite the Cout's disclaimers, they felt that this was a further secularization of the public school. Others hail the decisions as a victory for the maintenance of separation of the church and state.

The following implications of the ruling on the place of religion and public education were suggested in the January, 1964, *Bulletin of the Board of Parish Education:*

1. It was one thing to be friendly disposed toward Bible reading in the public school while it was permitted or required by law. In the light of the Supreme Court ruling, we should encourage compliance with the ruling.

2. We should continue to be sympathetic to public school teachers and administrators in their problem of dealing with religion in the public school program. The public school is not and cannot be a Christian school or a religious school. We should work with public school educators to define the proper role of the public school in teaching about religion.

3. We should stress the function of the church in teaching religion. The religious school founded and supported by the church remains the school where worship and the study of religion for commitment can be carried out. The Christian school remains the best agency for Christian education. For children attending the public school, the church must bend every effort to develop effective programs of Christian education in Sunday schools, weekday schools, and vacation Bible schools.

4. The importance of the home in Christian education must be emphasized. The church must help parents recognize that the Christian home is a Christian "school," and that they are teachers in that school. We must devise ways of helping parents meet their high responsibility as Christian teachers of their children.[12]

Released Time

The released-time program, begun in this country in 1913 in Gary, Indiana, was an imaginative cooperation between the public schools and the churches. It provided for regular instruction on the school premises for most of the day and the release of children to attend classes at their respective churches if the churches of the city would cooperate and provide such classes. The idea met with a varied acceptance. In some places there was a great deal of apathy, in others there was outright opposition, and in still others there was wholehearted cooperation.

Estimates vary as to the number of communities that had the released-time plan in operation. Dr. Erwin L. Shaver estimated that in 1952 the number of Protestant children alone enrolled in released-time classes was close to two million. At the National Conference on Weekday Religious Instruction in June, 1956, conservative estimates indicated that three thousand communities in forty-five states had some kind of program of weekday classes and that approximately three million children were enrolled in such classes.

The practice of conducting released-time classes in public school buildings was questioned by the *McCollum* case. Then, the decision of the United States Supreme Court in the *Zorach* case opened the door for widespread extension of the programs for weekday religious education on released time. (See Chapter 3.) The Lutheran Church-Missouri Synod has repeatedly encouraged released-time instruction. The 1956 Convention of the Synod adopted the following resolution on released time:

> *Resolved,* (a) That we commend those congregations which operate released-time schools and encourage all congregations, where local conditions permit, to make use of this agency also in their effort to increase the opportunities of more children for religious instruction; and be it further
> *Resolved,* (b) That congregations that cannot conduct a released-time school be encouraged to provide additional time for Christian education in classes conducted outside of school hours.[13]

The suggestion that congregations that cannot provide additional time for Christian education conduct classes outside of school hours has led to the development of extended weekday sessions after school and of Saturday schools. Some congregations in the Missouri Synod use both of these methods.

Shared Time

The idea of shared time or dual enrollment has recently been proposed as a way of dealing with several problems in the field of religion and education. Shared time is a relatively new idea, and we do not have any large-scale evidence of how the idea would work out in actual practice. Undoubtedly the idea has greater possibilities for some geographic areas than for others.

It is clear that in addition to fairly complicated administrative problems, the church-related schools also have other problems in the use of shared time. If the sponsors of church-related schools are sincere about the desirability of the Christian point of view being emphasized in the total curriculum, there is some question of how much instruction without this Christian point of view should be included. Obviously it would be helpful financially to have the public school provide the facilities and the teachers for such subjects as physical education, industrial arts, and home economics, even if the Christian point of view could be better emphasized in these areas in a Christian school. In such basic content areas as science, however, the church would have a very real problem in justifying its lack of interest in them on the basis that it does not matter whether instruction is offered under specifically Christian auspices or under the auspices of the public school.

The problem of the support of church-related schools is also involved in the consideration of shared time. The church-related school requires from the membership of the church the willingness to accept the value of the experience of general education within the framework of religious truth. Whether or not parents and church members will be willing to support as well the partial program of Christian education remains to be seen.

There is no doubt that the shared-time proposal would provide a way of paying part of the cost of education now borne by the patrons of nonpublic schools and would also eliminate the need for these schools to receive state funds. Church schools that are having difficulty financing their programs will undoubtedly find this a welcome relief. It remains to be seen what various communities will do with the possibility of shared time. Undoubtedly it has the potential of providing better Christian education for some pupils. Undoubtedly it can ease the financial cost for the sponsors of church-related schools. As various experiments in shared time are undertaken, it will be easier to appraise the program.

Government Support of Church Schools

When the principles of religious liberty, pluralism, separation of church and state, and cooperation are applied to the specific problem of government support of church-related schools, it is understandable that individuals and groups will have different opinions. On this particular topic every larger group can very likely register a variety of opinions from its membership. At this point these different opinions are affecting legislation in process. Should federal aid ever be made available to church schools, each group sponsoring a school would have to determine its own course of action.

The state of Connecticut in 1818 established the principle that state funds for education "shall be inviolably appropriated to the support and encouragement of the public, or common schools, throughout the state and no law shall be made, authorizing federal funds to be diverted to any other use than the encouragement and support of public or common schools." Other states followed the example of Connecticut so that by either constitutional provision or legislative act the use of public funds for religious schools, the teaching of sectarian doctrines in the public schools, or a combination of these is prohibited in certain states.

The Supreme Court in the *Everson* case, the *McCollum* case, and the *Zorach* case also addressed itself to this matter. In the *Everson* case, the Court asserted: "No tax in any amount, large or small, can be levied to support any religious activities or institutions, whatever they may be called, or whatever form they may adopt to teach or practice religion."

The book, *The State and Non-Public Schools*, published by the Office of Education, defines public and nonpublic schools in the following manner:

A "public" school is the creature of the State and is subject not only to the state's regulatory controls but is under the immediate operational control of a governmental agency or agent. A "public" school is supported and maintained at public expense.
A "non-public" school, while subject to pertinent regulatory controls of the state, is under the immediate operational control of a private individual or organization. A "non-public" school exists apart from the public school system of the state. It may be operated as a church-related or non-sectarian institution. It may be operated on a profit or non-profit basis. A "non-public" school is generally supported by private funds as distinguished from public funds raised by taxation.[14]

The First Amendment cannot be interpreted as forbidding any kind of aid to pupils attending church-related schools. The *Everson* case approved reimbursing parents for the cost of transporting children. Other benefits for pupils in nonpublic schools include free distribution of regular textbooks to children, free lunches and surplus milk, National Defense Education Act loans for equipment, and federal equipment acquired under the Surplus Property Act. As to whether or not the federal government may aid parochial church-related schools directly, the Congress will have to decide the question on the basis of its understanding of the application of these principles to particular situations. The Elementary and Secondary Act of 1965 does not give direct aid to nonpublic schools.

The Point of View of the Lutheran Church-Missouri Synod on State Support of Church Schools

In 1944 the Lutheran Church-Missouri Synod adopted a policy on state support of church schools which distinguished between state aid for the social-service program and for the teaching program of the schools. It was pointed out that the social-service program includes such matters as library service, lunches, health service, transportation, and other matters. It was held that the teaching program deals with the curriculum, the actual teaching, and the philosophy of education, and that a vital difference exists between these two programs. The position was taken that the social-service program should in equity be available to all children of school age irrespective of their school association, like public library service. However, the position was taken that it was most unwise for the church to accept a subsidy for the teaching program even though the right to control had been waived by the state. In fact, far from agitating for state support, the Synod decided to oppose the granting of state funds for sectarian use.

This policy was reaffirmed by the Synod at the 1947, 1950, and 1953 conventions. In 1953 it was resolved that this position be reaffirmed until such a time as new developments make a reappraisal of its position desirable or necessary. The nation-wide discussion of federal aid to education in March, 1961, prompted the Board of Parish Education to develop a statement on federal aid to church schools. This position reaffirmed in the perspective of federal aid the position adopted at the 1944 Convention.

The Synod also made several other resolutions. It went on record as opposed to federal loans for the construction of church-related elementary and secondary schools. To provide some relief for parents who paid educational fees, the Board of Parish Education suggested that the federal and state governments should permit parents who send their children to private or church schools to include tuition paid to these schools under contributions to religious, charitable, or educational purposes on their income-tax returns. Further, the Synod opposed "allowance for tax credit" for the full cost of the school tuition. And it also urged all its members to study and evaluate legislation coming before the various state legislatures and the Congress with respect to state or federal aid to church schools and to take the proper action.[15]

The subject of federal aid to education was again dealt with in the report of the Board of Parish Education to the 1965 Convention. In response to this report the Synod adopted the following three recommendations:[16]

> *Resolved*, That federal aid for children attending nonpublic schools, as authorized by the Congress and defined by the courts, be deemed acceptable so long as it does not interfere with the distinctive purposes for which such schools are maintained; and be it further
> *Resolved*, That synodical and District officials be requested to explore with appropriate government officials the availability, utilization, and administration of federal funds on an equitable basis for children attending nonpublic schools; and be it finally
> *Resolved*, That congregations faced with a decision regarding federal aid for children attending Lutheran schools be urged to consult with appropriate District officials.

This position represents a tested consensus in the Lutheran Church-Missouri Synod. It does not represent a unanimous point of view, however, because some members of the Synod have had and still have different opinions on this controversial matter.

The Child-Benefit Theory

In essence, the point of view of the Lutheran Church-Missouri Synod on the legitimate nature of support for the social-service program of the schools is based on the child-benefit theory. This theory suggests that certain kinds of public aid to children attending nonpublic schools are permissible because the aid is directly to the child and only incidentally to his school.

George R. LaNoue summarizes the situation on the child-benefit theory in these words:

> So, although the "child benefit" theory can be used to argue for text books, school transportation, school lunches, and medical services for parochial school students, the theory with the limitations the Court has put on it cannot be used to cover the major needs of parochial schools, teacher salaries, class room construction and facilities. Public aid for education in the future is not needed for children or parents but for schools. As Hughes in *Cochran* and Black in *Everson* made clear, aid for parochial schools themselves cannot come from public funds.[17]

LaNoue pointed out that under the child-benefit theory and the *Cochran* and *Everson* cases, the line of constitutionally permissible aid in the Court's opinion did not extend beyond these limits:

1. The aid went directly to the child or to the parent. No public funds went to the parochial schools directly or indirectly.

No religious organization or school acquired new property because of state action.

2. None of the books or the process of transportation could be adapted or used for the teaching of religion.

3. The state kept complete control of the administration of all state funds. In *Cochran*, the state chose the books and lent them to the children, making no special arrangements for those books used by children attending parochial schools. In *Everson*, the local public authority made the rules and contracts for transportation, and the children rode on regular buses operated by the public transportation system. It would be a different matter entirely to suggest that the court allow public funds to be turned over to the church schools to buy books or buses.

LaNoue concluded that a line can be drawn between permissible aid to the children and unconstitutional aid to the school.[18] He suggests three legal principles, which in his opinion would safeguard church-state separation and provide a just and politically useful solution to the problem of the benefits desired under the child-benefit theory. These are the following:

1. No religious institution may acquire new property through the state action of giving aid. The aid should go directly to the child or to the parents.

2. The state keeps complete control of the administration and spending of all public funds.

3. No religious use may be made of what the state provided.[19]

If these three limitations are accepted as legal principles, in Dr. LaNoue's opinion, then the child-benefit theory can be used to permit the state to include children attending parochial schools in its general concern for citizen health and safety through extension of medical and dental care and bus transportation within a general constitutional framework of separation of church and state.

The position of the Lutheran Church-Missouri Synod has been in support of the child-benefit theory. Despite voices that charge that this position is too restricted and that the church should request financial aid for the instructional program, and despite voices which emphasize that this position is too liberal and that no support from the government should be received for any aspect of the educational program of the church, this position remains for the time being the tested consensus of the Lutheran Church-Missouri Synod. In the light of Dr. LaNoue's suggestions, this position could be advanced also by other groups and individuals in the dialogue concerning federal and state aid for church-related schools.

Chapter Seven

•

TAX SUPPORT FOR RELIGIOUS SCHOOLS: A CATHOLIC'S VIEW

ROBERT F. DRINAN, S.J.

To every Christian who believes that the mission and message of Jesus Christ is carried on by some form of organized church, education is virtually inseparable from religion. To restate this truth is merely to reiterate what the unbroken tradition of Christian thought and centuries of Christian practice reveal and confirm.

In the modern world the Roman Catholic has seemingly a deeper belief in the inseparability of religion and education than do most non-Catholic Christians. This phenomenon is attributable to a variety of reasons to be explored later, but the traditionally close bonds which religion and education have had in the Western world must be frequently recalled if contemporary tensions and controversies surrounding the question of the place of religion in education are to be understood.

Father Drinan is Dean of the Boston College Law School in Boston, Massachusetts. He has written and lectured widely on issues involving civil rights, and he is the author of *Religion, the Courts and Public Policy*, McGraw-Hill, 1963.

The traditional Catholic belief has been that the Catholic Church and the parents of children share together the primary right to educate the young. Catholic educational philosophy would therefore be reluctant to concede that the state as such has any power or right to teach Catholic children in its own name. This is not to say, of course, that society rather than the state does not have the right and the duty to teach and to transmit those values on the maintenance of which the very survival of society depends.

It is furthermore hardly an exaggeration to state that for many centuries the Catholic Church was the mother of learning and probably the most influential and important source of both inspiration and financial aid for the development of education. In modern times the Church has been no less solicitous for education, but the modern world has experienced—at least since 1850—the double revolution which has brought about both compulsory education for all children and the inauguration by the state itself of a secularized, tax-supported school system which, because it is nonsectarian, is commonly assumed to be benevolently neutral to religion and hence acceptable to all students. Yet until about 1850 Christians and Jewish religious bodies were almost the sole educators of Western man.

It is against this background that the attitudes of the Catholic Church in America regarding the place of religion in education must be viewed. The millions of Catholics who came to America in the second half of the nineteenth century were simply not prepared to accept the public school, which at that time tended to be an institution with a pan-Protestant orientation.

Having set forth this very sketchy outline of a vast subject, let us discuss the profound and perplexing problems which confront Catholic educators and Catholic parents in contemporary America. The major problems can be grouped under the following categories:

1. American educational policy and the Catholic schools up to the *Pierce* decision[1] in 1925.
2. Statutory and decisional law regarding tax support for Catholic schools during the period from 1930 to 1966.
3. Federal aid to education and Catholic schools, 1947 to 1966.

Catholic Schools During the Years 1850 to 1925

The number of Catholic primary and secondary schools established during the second half of the nineteenth century constitutes an impressive monument to the faith and the generosity of those countless Catholic leaders and Catholic parents who came to the decision that their conscience required them to establish with their own funds a school system different in orientation from the tax-financed public school.

Official Catholic policy in America has always directed that all Catholic children should, whenever possible, attend Catholic *elementary* schools; no such firmly held policy has ever been established with regard to attendance at Catholic high schools or Catholic colleges. One can argue persuasively, however, that it was not the directives of Catholic bishops that induced Catholic parents to enroll their children in such vast numbers in Catholic schools; it was rather the profound feeling experienced by Catholics in every generation of American life that the public school was either implicitly Protestant in ethos or was so silent about religion that it was in effect antireligious.

Some individuals within the recent past have lamented the fact that America did not some one hundred years ago remove all traces of religion from its public schools; such action, these individuals theorize, would have prevented the origin and growth of the Catholic school system, a development which in their judgment was undesirable. The removal of a religious atmosphere from America's public schools a century ago would have been, of course, practically a psychological impossibility for the people of an overwhelmingly Protestant society in which the belief was widely held that the future of Protestantism and that of Americanism were inseparably linked.

One of the truly startling facts of American history is the apparent ease with which Protestants a century ago generally handed over the function of education to the state. Such a surrender of a traditional right and duty of the Christian church did not happen in any nation of northern Europe, although Protestants in those lands were, as in America, in the ascendancy and in a position to form and fashion the fundamental policy decisions by which those societies would be governed.

The little-explored circumstances which led to the release of education to the state by the Protestant bodies in America more than a century ago make the constant and almost spectacular effort of Catholic groups to create and maintain more and more schools a dramatically visible and uniquely challenging phenomenon. It appears, moreover, that no numerically significant group of Protestants will within the foreseeable future come to the decision that there is a need for Protestant parochial schools. Catholic schools consequently will continue to be almost alone in their petition for some share of state or federal funds.

Another poorly explored area of American educational history is the series of events by which virtually every state in the union adopted a constitutional or statutory policy forbidding tax support from going to any sectarian institution. The stated purpose of such a policy was the prevention of a struggle between Protestant sects for public money for their own schools. The exclusion of Catholic schools from public support was one of the generally unstated purposes of the many "anti-aid" amendments adopted by most of the states during the last century.

It is a curious anomaly that, although the vast majority of states enacted the sternest laws forbidding tax support for church-related schools, these institutions were nonetheless accepted and accredited without any difficulty for the purpose of student compliance with compulsory attendance laws. While one can argue that there is no necessary inconsistency in these two positions, one must concede however that the fully accredited school disqualified for any tax assistance reflects something of the ambiguity in the educational philosophy of American society in the late nineteenth century.

The only attempt in American history to be absolutely logical about the role of the public vis-à-vis the private school was the attempt in Oregon, prompted perhaps by a certain post-World-War-I hysteria, to eliminate completely the existence of private schools. It is seldom recalled that this attempt was successful on a 1922 referendum ballot in which the voters of Oregon decided, by a margin of 115,000 to 103,000, to close *all* private schools and to oblige *all* children between the ages of eight and sixteen to attend a public school. In the famous lawsuit that resulted, a Catholic group, the Society of Sisters, and a nonsectarian military academy secured a judgment against Oregon's Governor Pierce from the Supreme Court of the United States in which that tribunal unanimously held that no state could outlaw private schools.

While the Oregon decision did not technically turn on constitutionally guaranteed parental or religious rights, the *Pierce* ruling has come to symbolize the Magna Carta of freedom for the nonpublic school in America. Since the Supreme Court's decision on this matter in 1925 there has not been any serious challenge to the right of private groups to conduct schools which, if they are substantially equivalent to the public school, can request and receive all the rights enjoyed by the public school—except tax support.

It may be that the *Pierce* decision contains by implication those principles which would justify not merely the constitutional right of a private school to exist but also the right of such a school to some assistance, even equal tax support, with the public school. This question was not litigated in the Oregon controversy, but there is more than a little truth in the remark that the *Pierce* decision, which prohibited the outlawing of private schools, may also have implicitly precluded the state from depriving these schools of the tax support to which they are entitled as quasi-public agencies carrying out one of the secular purposes of the state.

Although one could argue that the *Pierce* case was the first decision of the United States Supreme Court to erode the wall of separation between church and state, it has seldom if ever been so construed. For virtually everyone and, of course, particularly for the Catholic the Supreme Court's vindication in 1925 of the parental right to educate has always been a landmark decision. It has been in fact a monumental victory for individual liberty achieved by a Supreme Court courageous enough to reverse the result of a popular plebiscite.

The public policy adopted in almost every state of refusing tax support to sectarian schools was never really challenged by Catholics either before the *Pierce* decision or after it. Indeed it could be said that Catholics regarded the "no-aid" policy as not presenting any great difficulty and almost as an inevitable part of America's inherited legal and religious framework.

It is uncertain exactly why Catholics in America have never seriously challenged the states' policy which denies any tax support to nonpublic schools. It may be that Catholics generally felt that such a challenge would not be fair to non-

Catholics and/or that a challenge to such a firmly rooted policy would be ill-advised.

During every decade of the twentieth century American Catholic schools have enrolled about one-half of the Catholic elementary student population. The Catholic ideal of "every Catholic child in a Catholic school" has never been attained on any widespread basis. Such an ideal is perhaps unattainable until or unless tax support of a substantial nature is given to private schools. This conclusion leads us to our second major topic— the law and aid for Catholic schools in the era of 1930-1966.

Statutory and Decisional Law on Private Schools 1930-1966

A major landmark in the history of Catholic schools in America came in 1930 when the Supreme Court of the United States sustained the constitutionality of a Louisiana law that granted free secular textbooks to pupils in parochial schools. Once again, however, this directive, the *Cochran* decision, like the *Pierce* ruling, did not involve the First Amendment and did not reach any question of religious freedom. But the reasoning used in the *Cochran* opinion opens up the possibility of state aid for all the secular aspects of the educational program of nonpublic, church-related schools.

It is one of the anomalies of the story of Catholic education in America that the 1930 decision authorizing benefits for children in Catholic schools appears not to have stirred any interest in the possibility of state aid for Catholic schools on the part of Catholic parents or Catholic officials. No attempts were made as a result of the *Cochran* decision to bring about state or federal legislation which would make possible the limited financial assistance validated by the Supreme Court. Neither the economic depression of the thirties nor the surging enrollments in

Catholic schools in the years after World War II operated to induce Catholics to petition at the state level for the benefits which the Louisiana legislature had granted to the children in nonpublic schools in that state.

The only item for which Catholics have petitioned at the state level has been school bus transportation. This noneducational aid is now granted to *all* children, including those attending Catholic schools, in some twenty-two states. It has been denied to private school students in several other states and has not become an issue in several more. Whenever Catholic parents have sought to change the law or local custom regulating the availablity of bus transportation to children going to nonpublic schools, their efforts have invariably resulted in a public Catholic-Protestant controversy of no small dimension. Many Protestants—or at least Protestant ministerial groups— seem to fear that Catholic requests for bus transportation will be a forerunner of further requests for more substantial aid.

It was this fear which, among many other factors, led Mr. Arch Everson, a New Jersey non-Catholic plaintiff, to bring a now famous lawsuit. The *Everson* opinion, a five-to-four ruling of the United States Supreme Court handed down in February, 1947, is the only case in all of American history in which the nation's highest tribunal has even approached the question of tax support for Catholic schools. Contrary to many of the contentions of the proponents and opponents of state aid for sectarian schools, *Everson* settles little if anything about the questions that are crucially important in resolving the issue of the constitutionality of public support for private schools. Since, however, *Everson* is the only source from which the authors of statutory and decisional law on this question may receive enlightenment, a rather full discussion of this important ruling may be helpful.

If there was one thing which Mr. Justice Black desired to make clear and to emphasize in his majority opinion in *Everson*, it was the finding that the challenged New Jersey law, authorizing reimbursement to Catholic parents for school bus transportation, was "public welfare legislation." Mr. Justice Black sought to make clear beyond any doubt the following pattern of reasoning:

1. Public welfare legislation is peculiarly within the province of state legislatures and should be nullified by judicial decree only for the gravest reasons.
2. Public welfare legislation which is designed to confer a benefit upon a particular class of individuals may not confer or deny such a benefit to anyone because of his religious faith or the lack of it.
3. Such legislation does not violate the First Amendment to the Constitution if in carrying out its secular purposes it confers some incidental and unintended benefit upon religion.

It may be that some readers of *Everson* would dispute whether the foregoing three propositions express the full meaning of the majority opinion of Mr. Justice Black. In all candor one would have to reply that the *Everson* opinion, in its actual holding and particularly in its reasoning, is not entirely clear. The four dissenting justices in *Everson* see in the majority opinion the very implications which Mr. Justice Black expressly sought to preclude.

Equally confusing are the interpretations given to *Everson* by the Supreme Courts of the states of Washington, New Mexico, Oregon, Wisconsin, and Alaska. All these tribunals have disallowed the child-benefit theory in their own states and, without finding it necessary to reject *Everson*, have declared unconstitutional state statutes permitting bus transportation for children attending private church-related schools. Only the Supreme Courts of Connecticut and Maine have seen in *Everson* a guideline by which a state court can rule that a properly drafted law providing for bus transportation to parochial schools can be constitutional.

Despite what commentators and state courts have said about the meaning of *Everson*, the fact remains that this 1947 ruling, which affirmed *Cochran* by name, is still good law. It has not been overruled and has in fact been confirmed to some extent by the Sunday law decisions of the U.S. Supreme Court in May, 1961. Mr. Leo Pfeffer, a vigorous opponent of tax support for private schools, has expressed the implications of Mr. Justice Black's opinion in these words:

> When the *Everson* decision is coupled with the *Cochran* decision, they lead logically to the conclusion that the state may, notwithstanding the First Amendment, finance practically every aspect of parochial education, with the exception of such comparatively minor items as the proportionate salaries of teachers while they teach the catechism.[2]

Despite the fact that the *Cochran-Everson* line of decisions supports their position, Catholics have never sought at the state level to make parochial schools the beneficiaries of tax support along with public schools. This circumstance presents another anomaly in view of the position taken by official Catholic spokesmen in favor of some share of federal aid to education going to parochial schools.

It can be seen, therefore, that during the period from 1930 through 1966 virtually no statutory or decisional law developed with respect to tax support for sectarian schools, except the validation by the nation's highest tribunal of grants of secular textbooks and free bus transportation to children attending church-related schools.

The only state laws—aside from statutes conferring health and welfare benefits on children—enacted during the entire period of 1930 to 1966 designed to impart a significant educational benefit on pupils in church-related schools were laws enacted in Rhode Island in 1963 and in New York in 1965 under which science texts and materials would be loaned to children in nonpublic schools in the same manner as these items are available to students in public schools.

It should be clear, therefore, that neither Catholic authorities nor Catholic parents have ever petitioned in the state legislatures for any aid for their schools beyond those benefits which can rightfully be described as health and welfare aids which the state clearly intends for *all* children. Despite the undeniable fact that Catholics have not raised the issue of tax support for their schools at the state level, there is present in America a widely held view that Catholics have as their objective the attainment of complete tax subsidization for their schools. When non-Catholics begin a discussion of the place of the Catholic school with the assumption that total support is the goal of the Catholic Church, any meaningful discussion immediately becomes almost impossible. The allegation that Catholics desire complete parity for their schools has received some substantiation, of course, from the position of Catholic officials with regard to federal aid for nonpublic schools. To that much misunderstood and thorny topic we now direct our attention.

The Catholic Position on Federal Aid to Education

Although the Catholic Church has been involved in numerous misunderstandings in the course of American history, it may be that the present official position of the Church with regard to federal aid has brought about a lack of understanding between the American people and the Catholic Church which is the most serious of all the controversies in which Catholics in America have ever been involved. For the first time in the nation's history the country's Catholic leaders have taken a firm and seemingly unrelenting position with regard to a matter of federal legislation.

Let us review as thoroughly as possible the major phases of the struggle over federal aid to nonpublic schools.

Federal aid to education became an option for the American Congress for the first time during the 1930's. At that time one could have constructed a cogent case to the effect that the nation's schools would not become more than mediocre unless aid beyond that available from local and state sources became a reality. Legislation for federal aid to education was not, however, enacted during the depression. After the war years, during which little school construction was done, federal aid seemed more imperative. An upcoming tidal wave of first-graders added impetus to the momentum for federal aid (a proposal endorsed by both political parties from 1946 until the present day).

In 1945 the Catholic claim to some share in federal aid to education was asserted for the first time in American history. It came in the form of an endorsement of the Aiken-Mead bill, a proposal which would authorize the federal government to make allotments of funds directly to nonpublic schools in those states which are prevented by their constitution or their laws from aiding church-related institutions of learning. With this endorsement the Catholic case for some part of federal aid to education became a permanent and not easily resolvable part of the already complex problem of finding an equitable formula for the distribution of federal money to all of the countless school systems in America.

During the earliest days of the controversy over the place of the church-related school in any scheme for federal aid three possible solutions to the problem emerged. They could be stated as follows:

1. No federal money should go to any sectarian school—even if state law permits such a grant.
2. The federal money should be given to the states with the provision that they be permitted to distribute it according to their own laws and church-state traditions.
3. States should be required to allocate at least a small minimum to children attending church-related schools in order to provide for various health and welfare benefits.

No one of these formulas—or any other variant of them—was embodied in legislation until the passing of the Act of 1965, a summary of which is given in Chapter Four. Federal aid to education was stalemated for a complete generation for three reasons—the strong and persistent opposition of many to the whole idea in principle, the demands of many that federal aid go only to desegregated schools, and the unfortunate but undeniable fact that no workable church-state formula had been found by which the opponents and proponents of some tax support for church-related schools could harmonize or compromise their differences.

In all candor it should be said that the Catholic position has been the principal source of the church-state impasse. Of the more than six million children in church-related, nonpublic schools in America (some twelve per cent of the total school population) ninety-two per cent are students in Catholic schools. The other eight per cent study in Lutheran, Seventh-Day Adventist, Episcopal or other sectarian schools, groups which have generally renounced any claim to a share in federal aid for their educational programs. Some Orthodox Jewish groups constitute the only significant religious body other than Catholics which seeks federal aid for its schools.

Catholic spokesmen have never taken any position on the basic question of the need or the desirability of federal aid as such. The consistent position of Catholic officials has been that *if* federal aid is granted, then some share should in justice be allocated to every eighth child in America, who attends a Catholic school.

It may well be that Catholic authorities would help themselves and would bring some clarification to the situation if they specified a certain amount or suggested a particular formula by which the Catholic claim could be satisfied. Catholic thinking, however, has not developed to this point; the Catholic request is simply that *some* appropriate share of federal aid be given to private schools to assist in financing the instruction in secular subjects which is imparted in these schools.

It may well be also that Catholic spokesmen would ease church-state tensions if they gave some indication of how vigorously and how persistently they expect to struggle on behalf of what they deem that justice requires with respect to aid for Catholic schools. On this point, however, once again Catholic thought has not developed to the point where a clear statement can be made. What is clear is that Catholic officials are aware of the fact that the advent of federal financing for the nation's schools may within a relatively short period shift the center of financial resources for education from the local and state level to the federal government. Therefore Catholic leaders have sought to prevent the adoption by the national government of the policy, enacted by the states in the last century, of giving tax support to public schools alone.

Catholics have argued vigorously on behalf of their case for some share of federal aid for Catholic schools. Although the

Catholic claims were advanced during the years of the Truman and Eisenhower Administrations, the Catholic plea for aid was spotlighted in the year 1961, when the nation's first Catholic President took the position that any aid to a church-related school of less than collegiate rank would be unconstitutional. The Catholic position on education in general and the structure and mystique of Catholic schools were understood more clearly during 1961 than ever before. It is uncertain how many persons previously uncommitted on the question of the desirability of aid to parochial schools were influenced by the unprecedented debate and dialogue that took place during the first two years of the Kennedy Administration.

Federal aid to education was not enacted, of course, until 1965, and it was expected that some publicists would attribute its earlier defeats to the position of the Catholic Church. Such a conclusion is only partially correct, but it nonetheless causes any Catholic who is devoted to the national welfare to be deeply concerned that a Catholic claim or plea may possibly have obstructed too long the fulfillment of some legitimate and indeed imperious national need.

Some small measure of fulfillment was given to the Catholic claim in the enactment of the National Defense Education Act in 1958. Under this bill, passed during the nation's post-Sputnik panic, nonpublic schools were made eligible to receive loans—not grants—for specific educational purposes deemed by Congress to be important to the nation's defense efforts. Although the aid made possible for private schools is minimal, its availability was at least a sign that Congress in 1958 did in fact realize that in the preparation of a bill to improve the nation's educational opportunities it would be more advisable to aid *all* children who go to school rather than to give assistance only to the public school.

Although Catholics urge, as noted above, that the Supreme

Court in *Everson* supports rather than opposes the case for public support for secular educational purposes, the principal Catholic arguments are not merely legal. Catholics argue that their religious freedom, which, along with the separation of church and state, is guaranteed by the First Amendment, should not be restricted by laws that virtually compel many of them to send their children to the religiously neutral or even secularistic public school.

Even if one disagrees with the premises and the conclusions of this argument, one should admit that the Catholic parents who employ this line of reasoning do have a grievance and a point of view which must be thoroughly discussed and, if possible, yet resolved. What angers Catholics most and what deepens their sense of injustice is the sometimes cavalier manner in which their entire position is dismissed as almost unworthy of discussion and patently untenable. Moreover, both Catholics and their adversaries must admit openly that the plea for public aid to church-related schools is based on a challenge to the dominance and hegemony which the public school has had in American society for over a century. Concessions to Catholic demands would not, of course, damage the public school in any way, but the granting of federal funds to nonpublic schools indicates the adoption of a philosophy of education based on the concept that the public school has no right to be the only publicly financed method of education at the primary and secondary level.

Catholics also point to the fact that the federal and state governments in many ways assist church-related groups in their secular or public-welfare activities. In fact *all* religiously affiliated organizations are eligible for aid when they conduct public service activities such as hospitals, homes for the aged, and institutions for handicapped youth. The state, in other words, maintains a friendly alliance with all church bodies in all of their secular activities except that of primary or secondary education.

Indeed the federal government by the Higher Education Facilities Act of 1963 made an unprecedented entrance into an arrangement by which *all* the colleges of the nation—public, private, and church-related—may receive substantial grants for the construction of facilities to be used for scientific purposes and for the erection of libraries. To deny that this college-aid bill has some relevance to the question of the constitutionality and the wisdom of federal aid to church-related schools of less than collegiate rank seems to be unrealistic.

We can deal, however, with three of the issues or proposals which in 1964 and 1965 dominated the discussion about federal aid and church-related schools. These issues were:

1. The feasibility of shared time.
2. The extent to which the public school had been secularized by recent Supreme Court decisions outlawing religious exercises.
3. The implications of the doctrine of governmental neutrality toward religion, which has been enunciated by the Supreme Court on several occasions in recent years.

Although each of these issues is most complex, let us discuss them with particular emphasis on their relevance to the question of federal aid for Catholic schools.

Shared Time

During the height of the national controversy in 1961 about federal aid and church-related schools the proposal of shared time was made by sincere and thoughtful non-Catholics who desired to effect some accommodation between the *status quo* and the needs of Catholic schools.

Several Protestant bodies have approved of shared time as a possible partial solution for the problems of the Catholic school. Catholics, while never refusing to discuss and to negotiate about shared time, appear to feel that this proposal has a rather limited potential for resolving the problems confronting Catholics. Many Catholic educators, however, are becoming involved in experimental programs of shared time—or "dual enrollment" as it is now sometimes called—and have a great deal of hope that the idea of shared time may flower into some significant programs which will ease the urgency of the financial plight of not a few Catholic schools.

The Secularization of the Public Schools

A vast number of American parents have apparently approved of the long-established customs by which some small religious orientation has been made a part of the classroom atmosphere of the public school. The vehement national protests over the Supreme Court's opinions in 1962 and 1963 outlawing the recitation of a state-composed prayer and the reading of the Bible in public schools indicate that countless parents think that some recognition of the role of religion is proper in the tax-supported school. Some of these individuals have endorsed the more than one hundred proposals in Congress to reverse the Supreme Court's decisions and to restore prayer and Bible reading to the public school.

For Catholics and for many others it is difficult to understand how the presence or absence of almost momentary devotional exercises has any significant effect on the curriculum or the orientation of the public school. But heat and controversy generated over this issue may lead to a deeper understanding of what the Catholic parent is trying to communicate when he

argues that the public school unwittingly operates on an ide-
ology of secular humanism.

At this time Catholic educators and jurists are pondering
what position they should assume amid the controversy over
attempts to restore devotional exercises to the public schools.
Catholics do not want to give additional impetus to the
Supreme Court's proscription of the influence of religion; at
the same time it is difficult for Catholics and for many others
to see how the Supreme Court could have, in a religiously
pluralistic society, done anything but exclude the religious
symbols of all faiths from the publicly financed school.

The nature and extent of the secularization of the public
school will almost certainly remain one of the key issues in
every future discussion about the advisability of giving tax
support to nonpublic, church-related schools.

Governmental Neutrality Toward Religion

For many commentators on the Supreme Court's opinions
on church-state matters the whole view of the Court can be
stated in the dictum that since state must be neutral toward
religion, it cannot aid religion directly or indirectly. Such an
interpretation can be justified by many citations from the
Court's opinions. But it is an interpretation which does not
reach the *real* issue, i.e., can the state carry forward its purposes in such a way that it accommodates itself to the parallel
purposes of religious organizations?

The whole thrust of Supreme Court opinions cannot be
summed up in the one concept of neutrality. The Court has
issued other principles that must be harmonized with the concept of neutrality which is admittedly so prominent in Supreme

Court thinking. Among these principles are the following:

1. The state must accommodate itself to the spiritual needs of its people. This norm was set forth in 1952 and has never been repudiated; it was the controlling principle by which the Supreme Court reached the view that released-time religious education, when conducted off the school premises, was a permissible adjustment of the state's schedule to the religious feelings and needs of its citizens.

2. The state has a positive obligation to respect and even to foster religious freedom. This principle was forcefully advanced by the Supreme Court in a June, 1963 decision in a case involving a woman of the Seventh-Day Adventist faith. In a most significant ruling the United States Supreme Court reversed the Supreme Court of South Carolina and held that a person unable to work on Saturday because of religious convictions could not be denied unemployment compensation if the sole reason for her unemployment status was her religious scruple against working on Saturday. Although the implications of this decision have still not become apparent to the public, the *Sherbett* opinion may well become a monumental ruling.

Therefore it will be seen that the church-state views of the Supreme Court cannot be summarized in the one notion of neutrality or the deceptive dictum of "no aid to religion." The government must accommodate itself to the religious needs and preferences of its people and, in addition, must provide for the protection and even the advancement of religious freedom.

Hence the solution to the conundrum of federal and state aid to Catholic schools will not be forged from one single legal or constitutional principle. Nor will it necessarily be fashioned only from principles which are now a part of the American dialogue on church-state controversies. Even the 1965 legislation is a questionable measure and poses problems to its administrators.

Catholics in America are very aware of the difficulties inherent in their position on federal aid and Catholic schools. They are likewise very sensitive to the fact that many sincere non-Catholics are basically opposed to the Catholic outlook on education and the Catholic claim to some share of state aid to assist them in the secular or nonreligious aspects of their educational programs. All that Catholics and many others are anxiously seeking to do is to create a climate of opinion in which the true dimensions of a religiously pluralistic society can be understood and appreciated. Once this climate of opinion is created the conscientious objections of all religionists will be so respected that there will be a fuller religious freedom for everyone.

Chapter Eight

•

REFORM JUDAISM AND EDUCATION

ALEXANDER M. SCHINDLER

The American Jewish community's approach to the complex of problems encompassed in the phrase "religion and education" can best be understood as the effect of an interplay of inner and outer forces, of the ideal and the real, of Jewish theology and Jewish history; it is the product of a people's faith shaped by its experience.

The monism which characterizes Judaism, its steadfast insistence of God's unity and its attendant unitary conception of human nature, clearly calls for the most comprehensive understanding of education's role, for the summary dismissal of any effort to compartmentalize it into well-defined, only thinly-related segments labeled "secular" and "sacred." On the other

Rabbi Alexander M. Schindler is Director of Education of the Union of American Hebrew Congregations, holding primary responsibility for the development of Reform Judaism's program of religious education. In addition, Rabbi Schindler heads the national policy-making body for religious education within Reform Judaism.

hand, the life experience of Jews, their persecution in lands where church and state were one and the whiplash of anti-Semitism which they and their children were made to feel in state religion-oriented schools, have made them espouse the ideal of the "secular" public school and thus to qualify the concept of education which comes from their faith.

Hence Jews stand in the vanguard of the struggle to maintain the principle of separation wherever church and state meet on the American scene. They resist the intrusion of denominational instruction and observances in the public classroom even as they oppose with vigor the assignment of public funds to church-established schools. At the same time, their essentially religious world view leads them to understand that not all religious concerns can be excised from the public school curriculum, that every system of education worthy of the name must strive to awaken awareness of life's spiritual dimension and foster devotion to its values. American Jews are confident that the public school can serve these ends without invoking the sectarian symbols and sanctions of institutional religion, without transmitting the teaching and forms of even those great faiths from which our spiritual and moral values are ultimately derived.

Judaism's View of Education

Because it is one of the oldest religions of mankind, its adherents scattered through all the world and their faith challenged by many varied winds of thought, Judaism is not a simple faith. It is, rather, a complex system of life and thought, embracing many points of view and distinctive only in its totality, in the singular integration of diverse details. Thus, there is no single Jewish philosophy of education; the religious literature of the Jew sounds many variations on the theme.

Still, a leitmotif can be perceived among the descants, allowing us to speak of a Jewish view of teaching and of learning.

Central to this view is Judaism's concept of man, which holds his nature to be a blending of body and soul, of matter and of spirit. Man is made of the dust, yet there is something in him which has its source in the divine and enables him to achieve communion with it. Because he was fashioned in the image of God, he can encounter God, if only he seek Him. "Man is not cut off and isolated from the universe, but a part of it. Somehow he can reach out and understand it. Man may be limited and small, but he can grow toward God because something in him corresponds to God."[1] The realization of this potentiality latent within him, the attainment of communion with the divine, constitutes man's essential task; it is the infinite duty which has been laid on finite human life.

Education is a principal means for life's fulfillment; "a man needs to study, so that he may become himself."[2] The unlearned man can never be pious; he may will to find God, but he does not know the way; he perceives the design, but he lacks the tools and has failed to master the craft. Learning is the key to the universe. Man becomes God-like, holy as God is holy, only as he grows in the knowledge of His world and Word.

Education is a means, not the end. Though prizing knowledge above all earthly possessions, Judaism ascribes no worth to study for study's sake alone. "He who has knowledge of the Torah but no fear of God, is like the keeper of a treasury who has the inner keys, but not the outer keys. He cannot enter."[3] The goal of learning is the refinement of a sensitivity to the divine; the beginning and the end of wisdom is the fear of heaven.

Judaism's conception of human nature is essentially unitary. It speaks of body and of soul but sees them bound in indissoluble union. Certainly the body is not burdened with all sin, nor is the soul given credit for all virtue.

> To what may this be compared? To a king who owned a beautiful orchard which contained splendid figs. Now, he appointed two watchmen therein, one lame and the other blind. One day the lame man said to the blind, "I see beautiful figs in the orchard. Come and take me upon thy shoulder, that we may procure and eat them." So the lame bestrode the blind, procured and ate them. Some time later, the owner of the orchard came and inquired of them, "Where are those beautiful figs?" The lame man replied, "Have I then feet to walk with?" The blind man replied, "Have I then eyes to see with?" What did he do? He placed the lame upon the blind and judged them together. So will the Holy One, blessed be He, return the soul to the body and judge them as one.[4]

Man is not a loose federation of two or even three separate states—body, mind, spirit—but rather is a composite of these correlative principles of being.

The implications of this conception for the understanding of education's task are clear. Its function is all-encompassing. It cannot be divided in any manner or restricted in any fashion. One cannot refine the competence of mind while oblivious to the needs and potentialities of body or blind to the values and final purposes which are born of man's spirit. The development of the total man is every teacher's concern. All life is education's proper province.

Judaism's reluctance to ascribe a final duality to human nature extends to the nature of man's universe. Here too, no artificial divisions are made, no realms sequestered from the horizons of inquiry which a man can properly pursue. "There is no not-holy, there is only that which has not been hallowed, which has not yet been redeemed to its holiness."[5]

The history of the Jews reveals no parallel to the warfare of theology with science which mars the history of Christendom.

Scientific inquiry was usually encouraged and given free rein. As one example, a twelfth-century curriculum sets the following order of studies: reading, writing, Torah, Mishnah, Hebrew grammar, poetry, Talmud, philosophy of religion, logic, arithmetic, geometry, optics, astronomy, music, mechanics, medicine, and lastly, metaphysics.[6] The array of Jewish scholars who coupled knowledge of Jewish law and lore with equal competence in the sciences is impressive; the leading contributors to the development of Jewish theology invariably ranked among the foremost scientists of their day. Moses ben Maimon (usually called Maimonides) offers classic proof: he was Talmudist and philosopher, astronomer and physician; his mastery of rabbinics was sufficiently great to have future generations of Jews designate him as a "second Moses"; his philosophical writings, seeking to harmonize Judaism and Aristotelianism, reveal an equally excellent grasp of Greek thought; and his scientific works—two volumes on poisons and their antidotes, a book on sexual intercourse, essays on asthma, on hemorrhoids, on hygiene, and a commentary on the aphorisms of Hippocrates—were consequential enough to merit translation and republication throughout the eight centuries since they were first written, most recently in English, by Johns Hopkins University, on the occasion of a Maimonides anniversary.

The study of nature is not inimical to the pursuit of the religious life, so teaches Judaism; it is a pillar on which the life of faith rests; God can be known only through its free and unrestricted service.[7] The student of science ought never be hindered in his quest by theological presuppositions; the "Torah is not a code that compels us to believe in falsehoods."[8] A contradiction between the teachings of Judaism and the findings of science can only be apparent, never real, and calls for the careful reevaluation of both. Either may be at fault, tradition misunderstood or scientific method poorly applied, and if the conclusions of science prove correct, tradition must yield the point and modify its understanding of the Word.

Nothing which serves to expand the adventurous horizon of man's mind should be excluded from consideration in the life-long educative process. The science, the wisdom, the skills of the world are as significant to man as are the teachings of tradition. All are necessary if man is to fulfill the purpose inherent in life.

That purpose must be served. If it is not, knowledge, whatever its kind, is vain; "the end of the matter, all having been heard: revere God and keep His commandments, for this is the whole duty of man."[9] It is in this spirit that the modern Jew voices his prayer:

> O Lord, open our eyes, that we may see and welcome all truth, whether shining from the annals of ancient revelations or reaching us through the seers of our own time; for Thou hidest not thy light from any generation of Thy children that yearn for Thee and seek Thy guidance.[10]

When they speak these lines at their weekly Sabbath services, and when they translate into their lives, as they hopefully do, the ideal implicit in them, Jews keep alive the ancient prophet's dream, a dream superbly characteristic of Judaism's view of learning, which envisages man's future as a time when "the earth shall be full of the knowledge of God, as the waters cover the sea."[11]

Faith Tempered by Experience

This then is the compelling religious conception which governs Judaism's approach to education: study is a never-ending task in life, a vital means for its fulfillment. All realms of knowledge, not just religious disciplines, but the sciences of man and nature too, and the humanities, are encompassed by this mandate; and all learning must be made to serve the end of faith, this end alone, the principal object of being—to help the I encounter the Eternal Thou.

It is a conception which still holds sway for Jews, at least for those who define their Jewishness primarily in religious terms. Its modification, to which we alluded in the introduction, is not one of substance but one of detail; and it applied, in the main, to American Jews, whose recent history witnessed their mass migration from central Europe to America.

Jews were made to suffer grievously in the lands of their origin; their existence was in continuous jeopardy, their religious life severely circumscribed. Invariably, their persecution was most relentless where Luther's dictum, *cuius regio eius religio*, determined the relation between church and state, where rulers told the ruled how to worship God, and priests told rulers how to execute state affairs. By the time Jews came to these shores in substantial numbers, the alliance between Protestant dissent and secular humanism had yielded its richest fruit; the principle of religious freedom was well established, and the concept of voluntariness in matters of faith had become a cornerstone of American law. Here Jews found safety. Here they found freedom in a measure rarely matched in the two thousand years of their wandering. Little wonder that they attributed their liberties primarily to the principle of separation and that they are boldly zealous in its defense!

The sharp and comforting contrast between the·old and the new was strikingly manifested in the realm of public education. In Europe only a handful of Jewish children were granted admission to government-established schools; the lucky few who were thus chosen had to make a payment of blood for their privilege. They were subjected to stinging indignities, insulted and assaulted to remind them of their inferiority, to make them appreciate the gracious gift bestowed. Whatever the ultimate purpose, the state was hardly guiltless. State-appointed teachers condoned or even encouraged such incidents. These expressions of anti-Semitism invariably were cloaked in the garment of religious bigotry, given occasion by class prayers (always alluding to the Crucifixion), by school observances of festivals (Easter was ever a propitious time to resuscitate the blood libel), and by the caustic commentaries of teachers in interpreting the Biblical text. Not so in America! Here the Jewish immigrant found governmental schools whose doors were opened wide to welcome his children, whose teachers and administrators accorded them treatment fully equal to that extended to all other students. Again, the American Jew attributed his blessing primarily to the principle of separation, to the circumstance that the American public school had been divested of those denominational dimensions that so distressed him and his children elsewhere. Thus it was that American Jews became champions of the "secular" public school, learning to reverence it as a "precious gift to be passionately protected and preserved."[12]

Here we confront the modern-day modification of Judaism's traditional approach to learning. Today's American Jews recognize the worth of disjoining the educational process, conceding the possibility of its departmentalization into "secular" and "sacred" components.

The modification is modest indeed. It involves a peripheral change, not an alteration in essence. It constitutes a division of labor, as it were, and not a dichotomy of final purposes. The goals of education, public and private, remain the same. The public school can well serve religion's ultimate concerns without also teaching religion in any formal sense.[13]

Maintaining the Wall—Religious Observances

American Judaism offers substantial, unaccustomed unanimity in its approach to the many issues affecting the adjustment of church and state in the realm of public education. The response is uniform and unequivocal, always applying the principle enunciated by the highest court, "separation means separation, not something less."

Every ritual expression of religion in the public elementary and high schools is rejected on this basis, from the recitations of prayers to the devotional reading of the Bible, from the singing of sacred songs to the observance of sectarian festivals, not excluding joint religious celebrations.

Long before the Supreme Court rendered its decision in the *Engel* v. *Vitale* case, American Jews asserted that state laws requiring or permitting the recitation of prayers are wholly inconsistent with the Establishment Clause, even when these prayers are chosen for their "nondenominational" quality or composed with this intent in mind.[14] Moreover, to be true to its essential nature, prayer must be personal, particular, passionate; it cannot be neutral or detached. Here, Jews share fully the view of the late Paul Tillich, who holds the "unspecified affirmation of God" to be "irrelevant," a "rhetorical-political abuse" of religion in its finest sense.

> Politicians, dictators, and other people who wish to use rhetoric to make an impression on their audience like to use God in this (unspecified) sense. It produces the feeling in their listeners that the speaker is serious and morally trustworthy. This is especially successful if they can brand their foes as atheistic.[15]

The rote recitation of "neutral" prayers holds forth no hope for the attainment of a meaningful religious experience; it is form without substance, an empty gesture bereft of spiritual significance. Nor can such recitation, without further comment by the teacher or discussion by the class, be seen to serve the ends of character education; the expectation that the mechanical mouthing of prayer formulas will steel the moral fibre of the student runs counter to reason, counter to evidence, counter to all accepted theories of learning.

What is true for "neutral" prayer is true for nondenominational Bible reading, not when the Book is studied as part of a great literature course, but when it is ordered as a daily exercise in religious devotion. Such Bible reading as the latter virtually constitutes compulsory attendance at a religious service. Jews fear, further, that in this manner Christological ideas at variance with the Jewish understanding of the Bible will be transmitted to their children.[16] The Bible is not a nonreligious book, and the hypothesis that it is a nondenominational book must similarly be put to serious question.

> Theological difference among Protestants, Catholics and Jews have necessitated each group authorizing its own translation of the Bible. These theological differences resulted in frequent and prolonged controversies in the nineteenth century, when in numerous instances Catholics asked the courts to ban the readings of the King James Bible and when even Protestant groups fought among themselves as to which denominational translation should be declared non-denominational.[17]

Again, as in the use of prayer, the hurried, perfunctory recitation of texts can never further but only retard the advancement of both religion and moral education.

Jewish opposition to school observance of holy days—particularly the celebrations of Christmas and Easter, the singing of carols, the presentation of Nativity and Crucifixion plays, the display on school property of manger scenes—has been a cause of considerable community tension and of serious inter-religious misunderstanding. Hopefully, the preceding paragraphs have helped to clarify the issue somewhat by showing that a consistent application of the principle of separation makes this opposition essential.

After all, Christmas and Easter are religious holidays in the specific sense of the term. They are sectarian, denominational festivals. They celebrate the birth and death of Jesus, who is the founder of the Christian faith. The Nativity scene is a hallowed symbol of Christ's birth. Christmas pageants are representations in word and dance of profoundly religious, Christian ideas. And Christmas carols derive from the music of the church; their words have origin in its sacred liturgy.

Manifestly, Christmas and Easter are not national or cultural holidays, and thoughtful Christians should be as offended as are Jews by the effort to obscure or to diminish the theological content of their celebration.

> The fact that Christmas music is mixed with such other "holiday" music as "Rudolph, the Red-Nosed Reindeer" and "All I Want for Christmas Is My Two Front Teeth" in no way changes the situation. . . . If Christmas is a holy day of great religious importance, Christians should be the first to rebel against its vulgarization in the public schools. Indeed, many sensitive Christians have joined in the campaign to "Put Christ Back into Christmas." But it is with a sense of sadness that we observe how very few Christians have seriously objected to the cheapening of their sacred day.[18]

In a sense, Jews long for the restoration of at least some of the stern standards of colonial New England, whose Puritans prohibited the public celebration of Christmas, barred all "pomp and pagan revelry" in the observance of the day, and insisted that it be marked in conduct with a solemnity befitting Christianity's most holy hour.

The attempt to assuage Jewish sensitivity by instituting joint holiday observances fails in the desired effect. American Jews are particularly discomfited by the Christmas-Hanukkah union, which, principle aside, gives currency to a grave misunderstanding of their faith when it equates a relatively minor festival of Judaism with a feast of the greatest moment to Christendom. The springtime twin-observance is only slightly more appealing; Easter and Passover hardly strike a heavenly harmony of theme. But what is infinitely more important, a principle is at stake. And principle will not be compromised. Joint observances of religious holidays in public school are not less a breach of the American ideal than are the celebrations of a single faith.

Religious Education and the School Curriculum

The problem of religious instruction in the public school is vexing in its complexity, more intricate by far than are the issues of religious observance. Its ramifications are many and tangled, forming a Gordian knot which, so the better part of valor dictates, cannot be cut in a single bold stroke but must be unraveled with infinite patience and care.

Two possible approaches, both extreme, can readily be rejected and require no lengthy elaboration. Sectarian indoctrination on public school premises clearly constitutes a breaching of the wall between church and state. Indeed, it was ruled to be so by the court in the historic *McCollum* case. The opposite alternative, the elimination of all religious concerns from general school teaching, is neither desirable nor feasible. One simply cannot teach without transmitting some religious data. One cannot convey a full understanding of contemporary culture without at the very least recognizing religion's role in the making of its essential elements—its music, literature and art, its morals and its laws. This view, too, is supported by court opinion. In the *Schempp-Murray* majority decision, Justice Clark took pains to point out that the banning of devotional Bible reading and the injunction against the recitation of the

Lord's Prayer do not by any means imply that the study of the Bible for its "literary and historic qualities" or the study of religion "when presented objectively . . . as part of a secular program of education" constitute a violation of the First Amendment.

But the objective transmission of religion's historic contribution to civilization hardly qualifies as religious teaching. Can religion itself be taught in the public school—its tenets and its values—without partiality, without the substitution of indoctrination for learning? This the question that yields no ready answer and continues to trouble the waters of intergroup relations on the American scene.

A number of proposals in recent years aim to allow the teaching of religious tenets without doing violence to the principle of separation. They build on the assumption that there are fundamental principles of faith which all religions share, which can be isolated and organized in unit form and then transmitted as the common, nondenominational core of faith.

American Jews do not embrace such efforts with a full heart. Of course they agree that a common core exists, that the great religions of the world do hold many views in common. There is a place to allow for full cooperation between religions. However, Jews doubt that these tenets can be isolated from the context of the religious current without destroying their essential nature and without vitiating all that is spiritually meaningful in every faith. Religious ideas and their forms are inseparably intertwined. Both are sanctified by faith. The moment they are separated one from the other, form loses its essence and the idea is robbed of its force.

> Phrasing and style become supremely important and indeed matters of conscience, as is evidenced by the fact that chuches differ not as to the content of the Lord's Prayer, but as to its wording. There is not a single thought in that prayer to which

a devout Jew could take exception. Yet it is for him a Christian prayer which Jewish tradition and his own religious sensitivity enjoin him from reciting. It is only a person emancipated from religious tradition who speaks of forms as the "externals" of religion. How meaningful then can a common core of belief be that does not have the support of a tradition which includes symbols, memories, powerful emotional associations.[19]

More than this, once an idea is abstracted from one form and is cast in another form, the idea itself undergoes substantive change. When the principles of a faith are isolated from their tradition and combined with other principles similarly extracted, something entirely new emerges. Doubtless this is what the American Council on Education had in mind when it criticized the common-denominator plan on the ground that it "might easily lead to a new sect, a public school sect, which would take its place alongside the existing faiths and compete with them."[20] Rabbi Richard G. Hirsch, in his testimony before the Senate Judiciary Committee, makes this pertinent and incisive comment:

> Public school sponsorship of non-denominational religious exercises (and teaching) potentially establishes a new major faith—"public school religion." For a brief, but significant time during the school day, the school becomes a house of worship, the teacher becomes a religious leader, the class becomes a congregation, and the members of the school board are enshrined as founders of the new faith. How are the ritual, the theology, and spiritual heritage of the "new Public School Religion" determined? Through divine revelation and interpretation by theologians? No, by public boards, commissions and courts, elected or appointed through the secular, political process.

Still one other, more practical matter must be considered. Once such a common-core curriculum is actually developed,[21] how can we be certain that teachers will transmit this teaching without partiality toward their own religious commitment? Are we reasonable to expect teachers to suppress their own deep devotions and commitments? More important by far, and assuming for the moment that the impossible is possible, just what religious values would such objectivity in teaching yield? Proper religious instruction calls not for objective detachment but for passionate involvement. "There is no more ineffective way of teaching religion than to give an objective account of religious history. For this means robbing history of the inner meaning and specific elements of faith and truth."[22]

These arguments manifestly mitigate against all nondenominational or interdenominational religious education plans put forward thus far. This is the considered view of the American Jewish community on the subject.

> We are opposed to all attempts by the public elementary and secondary schools to . . . teach about the doctrines of religion. Without passing on the question whether such teaching is inconsistent with the principle of separation of church and state, we believe that factual, objective and impartial teaching about the doctrines of religion is an unattainable objective. Any attempt to introduce such teaching into the public schools poses the great threat of pressures on school personnel from sectarian groups and compromises the impartiality of teaching and the integrity of the public school educational system. Our opposition to such teaching rests on these grounds.[23]

If religious doctrines cannot be taught, what of moral and spiritual values? Can they be drawn from the matrix of religion which brought them to existence and be kept alive without continued dependence on their source?

Here, American Judaism voices a somewhat more optimistic view.

> Insofar as the teaching of "spiritual values" may be understood to signify religious teaching, this must remain, as it has been,

the responsibility of the home, the church, and the synagogue. Insofar as it is understood to signify the teaching of morality, ethics, and good citizenship, a deep commitment to such values has been successfully inculcated by our public schools in successive generations of Americans. The public school must continue to share responsibility for fostering a commitment to these moral values, without presenting or teaching any sectarian sources or sanctions for such values.[24]

This mandate is not easy to fulfill. It requires the delicate disjoining of the educative process, which, as indicated, historic Judaism did not deem possible, the abstraction of the ideal from its original form, the separation of ethical values from their life-giving tradition. American Judaism encourages this departmentalization only because of its profound regard for the secular public school, because of the school's ability to transmit religious values apart from denominational doctrine and without sectarian bias.

To be sure, spiritual and moral values cannot forever be maintained without reference to their source; faith is the necessary condition of their continuance; they gain their fullest dimension only when they are woven into the tapestry of a rich religious life. That is why Judaism insists on an intensive program of religious instruction in the synagogue and on the development of meaningful religious life-patterns in the home.

It might be noted, in this connection, that the *Zorach* decision did not end the Jewish community's unfavorable response to the released- and dismissed-time programs. The following objections are usually offered: such plans threaten the principle of separation; the amount of religious instruction which can be given in the time provided is negligible; more often than not, school authorities put pressure on students to attend religious school classes; those who refuse to be "released" are rarely if ever given meaningful general instruction; such programs serve to emphasize religious difference in a public arena; indeed,

Jewish children at times attend Christian classes for fear of disclosing their religious differences.

Be that as it may, the public school cannot be enjoined from transmitting ethical and moral concepts, however religious the origins. To begin with, these concepts cement our democracy. They form the faith of this land. Their preservation is vital toward the fulfillment of the American dream. Were we to keep our schools from fostering moral values, we would deprive them of their reason for being and then we might as well give up the enterprise of public education. A school which does not seek the moral development of its students is no school at all; all education worthy of the name is essentially education of character.

An Aid to Religion and a Challenge

What has been said concerning the proper goals of public education should serve to refute the charges that our schools are "godless," "atheist," and "antireligious," that they create, of necessity, an antagonism to faith and institutional religion. On the contrary, the spirit of religion, though not its forms, can animate the atmosphere with which the school surrounds its students. And in this atmosphere our children can grow, intellectually and spiritually, precisely in a manner in which we as religious people want them to grow.

When Jews espouse the cause of the "secular" public school, they do not use the adjective in its philosophical context. Our determined opposition to doctrinal instruction extends with equal force to the dogmas of scientific naturalism. We do *not* want the school to teach our children that reality is limited to the "seen," that empirical science and logic are the only proper tools in man's quest for knowledge. We do *not* want the school to teach our children that spiritual values are "purely subjective," that religion is thus but a branch of psychology, revealing the vagaries of man's mind and the caprices of his emotional life, and no more. Even as the teacher is debarred from teaching principles which presuppose the acceptance of religious doctrines, so is he debarred from teaching principles which presuppose the acceptance of antireligious doctrines.

"Secular," as the American Jewish community applies the word to the public school, means not "irreligious" but "nondenominational," "nonsectarian," intended for pupils of all religious persuasions, and even for those whose parents affirm no faith. What it means is that the state, enjoined by law from establishing any one religion, without endeavoring to provide for all education but leaving many of its essential aspects to church and home, attempts to give moral and mental training and instruction in secular subjects of consequence to all future citizens—the entire process being conducted in "an atmosphere of social idealism."[25]

Jewish opposition to doctrinal instruction in the public classroom rises in no small measure from the fear that such teaching, in attempting to meet the conflicting demands of competing religious groups, will not further but hinder the advance of religion. "We urge a broad interpretation of the first amendment precisely because we want religion. If we were truly secularists, we would encourage such things as non-denominational prayer in the public schools as a tool by which to make life and faith less sacred, less passionate . . . the worst thing that could happen to the churches and the synagogues would be to . . . [develop in the public schools] a religion which would consist of a set of meaningless, watered-down, non-sectarian platitudes."[26]

Thus, the problem of religious education can never be solved by shifting the burden of responsibility for its advancement from church to public education.[27] It will be solved only when church and synagogue recognize their full and final responsibility in this realm and take the matter of religious education much more seriously than they have.

> When organized religion spends more for religious education than for its choirs; when it plans its programs of religious education with the fervor with which it promotes evangelistic campaigns; when it is more proud of its schools than of the size of the congregation or the beauty of its architecture; when it selects ministers of education with the same care it chooses its preachers and when it invests its attempts at educating the young with the importance it ascribes to its weekly Sabbath service—then shall it have begun to cope with the problem of religious education.[28]

In this manner, the public school both aids and challenges the religious of America in their quest to transmit the heritage of faith. It aids the synagogue and church by fostering a devotion to the values which they share. It offers them challenge by imposing on them the duty to transmit the doctrinal beliefs and practices which give these values sanction.

The late President John F. Kennedy perceived this challenge and expressed it well when, immediately following the Court's announcement of the *Engel* v. *Vitale* ruling, he declared: "The Supreme Court has made its judgment. Some will disagree, others will agree. In the efforts we are making to maintain our constitutional principles, we will have to abide by what the Supreme Court says. We have a very easy remedy here, and that is to pray ourselves. We can pray a good deal more at home and attend our churches with fidelity and emphasize the true meaning of prayer in the lives of our children."

Chapter Nine

•

TEACHING ABOUT RELIGION AS A PUBLIC SCHOOL POLICY: SOME QUESTIONS

STANLEY E. BALLINGER

Teaching about religion has become a problem because of the kinds of answers the American courts and substantial segments of the public have given in discussing the more general question of the desirable role that religion should play in American public education.

The operation of the courts and of American public opinion has narrowed the range of choice which is legally permissible or socially practicable. This essay will not deal with the rightness or wrongness of this narrowing of choice. The net impact of the *McCollum* case, the Regents Prayer case, and the recent *Schempp* and *Murray* cases has been to declare prayers, Bible

Dr. Stanley E. Ballinger is Professor of Education at Indiana University. He has been visiting lecturer and professor at Yale, Teachers College of Connecticut, and the University of Southern California. He served as a Fulbright Lecturer at the Tokyo Gakugei University and as special lecturer at the American Seminar on Education in Kyoto, Japan.

reading, and other religious ceremonies or worship activities contrary to the Federal Constitution, the fundamental law of our land. There is considerable reason to believe that teaching *about* religion in some form or other is the main policy line left generally available for those who want to see religion given greater emphasis in the public schools. However, it may take a little time for some schools to stop defying the courts and bring their practices into conformity with Constitutional pronouncements.

Let me state a general position on the question at this point, with qualifications and reservations to emerge in the course of the essay: I believe that *the public schools can, should, and almost inevitably must teach about religion in their program.* But to say this is to raise a great many vexing questions. The statement leaves open for interpretation the more particular meanings for school policy and program. It is not the purpose here to develop a definite policy or plan for teaching about religion. What I shall try to do is to set forth more fully than is commonly done the character of the problem which is involved in the proposal to teach about religion in the public schools. The long-run acceptability of solutions to policy problems of this kind rests fundamentally upon the quality of the analysis which identifies the nature of the problem. It is with this point in mind that I hope to escape being justifiably charged with being excessively negativistic.

It has been observed above that the particular form of the problem which we face has been shaped by the law and the courts; I shall give no central attention to the problem of legality in this article, since this was discussed in Chapter Three. Further, it is a mistake for analysis to start too soon with legal questions. Schoolmen need to know what the law requires and what it forbids, naturally. Beyond that their thinking should address itself to the larger ranges of the process of determining the ethical and educational worth and justification of a given practice.

We have an old American custom of regarding questions about a man's religion as impertinent. Nonetheless, when a man discourses on the subject of religion, his listeners perhaps have a right to some clues at least as to his general standing ground on such matters. The essay itself will reveal much about my general approach to religion; but to begin with, let me say that neither formal creed nor membership in any organized church has any appeal for me, although my concerns overlap a great deal with those of individuals who do find creed and church a viable place for their commitments. As one who approaches questions within a framework of naturalism, I have trouble with the meanings of terms like "supernatural," "divine," and "transcendent faith." I regard speculations as to the ultimate nature of things as just that: speculative. It is undoubtedly true that considerations of ethics (in a secular, naturalistic setting) are basic in my thinking, not in the sense that I am more ethical than the next fellow, but in the sense that I find the ethical dimensions of problems interesting and significant. My perspective within this essay is derived essentially from considerations of *what education ought to be* on rationally humane grounds. The controlling criteria thus are generally philosophical and pedagogical rather than religious, although I regard myself as by no means insensitive to the claims of religion on all counts.

Protestant Atmosphere of the Public Schools

The discussion of the problems of religion and education in this country has been influenced, often toward obscurity of essential issues, by the fact that the American public school has tended to operate in an atmosphere of general Christian theism. More than that, its program has typically had strong Protestant overtones. The very meaning of the term "nonsectarian" in the context of religion and education has been shaped by the historical tendency to regard "sectarianism" as having to do with the hair-split variations of Protestant denominations. We cannot therefore equate in American usage the terms "nonsectarian" and "religiously nonpartisan." That is, many people apply the term "nonsectarian" to education in a way that cannot be taken to mean religiously "nonpartisan." Yet the controversy often is approached and positions are taken on the basis of this fundamental confusion. It is entirely likely that for understandable historical reasons Protestants have fallen into this error more commonly than Jews and Roman Catholics.

One has only to turn to such nineteenth-century schoolbooks as the McGuffey Readers to identify the generalized Christian theism that permeated the work of the common school. In a country where the cause of religious freedom has been promoted with so much agonizing sacrifice, it is perhaps a matter of surprise that almost no questions seem to have been raised as to this partisan approach to religion in the late-nineteenth-century common school, support of which had become involuntary through systems of public taxation. Further, it should be remembered that attendance at school had become compulsory in most states by 1900, with the common school the main practicable option for most children.

These observations on the general Protestant atmosphere of the American public school have been introduced at this point as a general precaution against the unwitting use of premises rooted in Protestant presuppositions. This would be too narrowly preferential for the public schools of a society with such a religiously diverse culture as ours.

Two Conceptions of Education

To consider the question of including religion in the public school program, we may find it useful to distinguish two general conceptions of education:

1. Education as the preservation and transmission of a body of traditional beliefs, practices, ideas, and attitudes.
2. Education as the provision of the younger generation with the resources and tools for the *intelligent reconstruction* of the complexly multiple heritages of cultural achievement evolved by past generations.

Perhaps the single most important generalization that can be made about the development of religious education in the United States from its beginning down to the present is that, almost without significant exception, institutionalized religious education has been of the first kind: conserving, uncritical, protective of the established order. While some forms of preferential sectarianism (religious partisanship) are broader or narrower than others, are there any pre-college programs of religious education which are not essentially indoctrinative: shunting the learner away from the avenues of free inquiry rather than opening them up for him? To the extent that this is an essentially valid picture, it is going to figure in important ways in what people mean by teaching the facts of religion or teaching about religion after four and a half centuries of indoctrinative religious education.

Two Countervailing Principles

For the sake of the present discussion, two principles are suggested, both of which I must embrace and which also have some claim on a larger range of acceptance. Taken together, they offer insight into the kind of problem which teaching about religion represents.

1. *The principle of cultural inclusiveness.* No significant segment of the culture should be automatically excluded from the field of learning of youngsters in school. Not everything is either possible or desirable for the public school to do at any one time or place, but I cannot see how we can validly suppress the ideally formulated right of the child to study all significant aspects of the culture within which his own life is to be lived and his destiny worked out. The decision of what to include or not to include ought to be a matter of prudential practicality; no area of learning ought to be proscribed as *ipso facto* undesirable.

2. *The principle of free inquiry.* Education is not indoctrination. Habits of critical inquiry and appraisal relative to the many possible ways to become a human being, to the many alternative modes of thought, commitment, and action open to modern man are to be seen as a primary dimension of an education worthy of a free and freedom-loving people. The problem of what to include in the public school program and questions of teaching and studying any particular matter should be approached with due consideration for the rules of rational inquiry and criticism.

In the abstract these two principles would seem to be quite compatible with each other, but as commonly interpreted in situations of controversy over religion and public education, one or both of these principles are violated by many of the proposals for the inclusion of religion in the public school program. A proposal to reduce the reference to religion to an absolute minimum seems to defy the child's right to study his culture in all its dimensions. On the other hand, religiously preferential programs such as Bible reading, prayer and worship services, and the like tend to contradict the principle of free inquiry. It would appear that in the question of religion and education there is a large bloc of people who in some sense do accept the principle of cultural inclusiveness, but there appears to be only a relatively small group who will accept the principle of free inquiry applied to the study of religion. It is not clear even that those who say that they accept the principle of freedom of inquiry in religious matters fully want to mean what they appear to be saying. Thus it would seem that many if not most proposals for dealing with religion in the public schools of the United States, including proposals for teaching *about* religion, are in effect, covertly or overtly, proposals to include religion in education on some kind of noncritical, preferential basis. This point will be more fully pursued in the pages that follow.

Let me try to summarize the essential significance of the foregoing remarks by posing the following question: With a public commitment to the ideal of free inquiry, how ought the public school to include within its program the study of the religious aspects of the culture when such study is perceived by most Americans as an enterprise primarily for the sake of securing the young unshakably in the ways and beliefs of their elders?

The Educational Policies Commission Statement

Lest it be thought that we are sparring with a straw man, it is appropriate at this point to introduce an actual statement of a policy position favoring teaching about religion in the public schools, a position which is fairly representative of many which have appeared during the last decade or more. A statement of this order which would enjoy considerable assent from the American public, including a great many professional educators, was made by the Educational Policies Commission in 1951:[1]

THE PUBLIC SCHOOLS CAN AND SHOULD TEACH ABOUT RELIGION

The public school can teach objectively *about* religion without advocating or teaching any religious creed. To omit from the classroom all references to religion and the institutions of religion is to neglect an important part of American life. Knowledge about religion is essential for a full understanding of our culture, literature, art, history, and current affairs.

That religious beliefs are controversial is not an adequate reason for excluding teaching about religion from the public schools. Economic and social questions are taught and studied in the schools on the very sensible theory that students need to know the issues being faced and to get practice forming sound judgments. Teaching about religion should be approached in the same spirit. General guides on the teaching of all controversial issues may be helpful. If need be, teachers should be provided with special help and information to equip them to teach objectively in this area.

Except perhaps for a kind of implicit optimism as to the ease with which this statement can be translated into the operational terms of school policy and classroom practice, I find nothing with which to disagree directly in the statement. The remainder of this essay will subject this general position to careful scrutiny to identify some attendant difficulties in the position. It should be clearly understood that, although my tone may often be critical, I am not in any sense arguing against the general position expressed in the Educational Policies Commission Statement. The problem does not lie in the overall acceptability of the statement; it lies in the *problems of meaning* that arise when one projects this statement as a normal guide onto the conditions of the public school programs.

The Problem of Defining Religion

In trying to deal meaningfully with a directive for policy and program in teaching about religion, one soon encounters a problem of defining the term "religion." The difficulties stem from the fact that religion is not, as most people see it, something to be expressed simply in factual or descriptive terms. It is what we might call a value-loaded term of the same type as the term "education." In other words, the definition of the term "religion" gets wrapped up with people's conflicting values, their sense of life commitment, and a whole tangle of "ought's," "should's," and "must's." Anthropological studies of cultures throughout the world point to the virtual impossibility of a descriptive definition of "religion" that will fit all societies. One is forced to retreat to generalities so vague that all useful meaning is lost, such as defining religion as "man's posture toward the unknown and unknowable." Where the label "religion" is held to apply to a thousand and one different and typically conflicting culture complexes, by what objective process does one identify a set of defining criteria? There is, of course, no simple answer.

The history of religion in the West bears ample witness to the general tendency to define religion in such a way that all or most religions except one's own are excluded. To define religion, for instance, as a mode of relationship between God and man excludes various forms of polytheism as well as all brands of nontheism. On the other hand, to define religion as that to which one gives his ultimate loyalties opens the door to the inclusion of Communism, various brands of ultra-nationalism, and other secular ideologies. Still again, to take the viewpoint of the man in the street and define religion as what the churches say it is, or some common denominator thereof, is to say that the unchurched may not claim a religion or a religious point of view.

Similar to the kind of problem we face here is the plight of the United States government, especially as it acts through the Supreme Court. In consideration of the protection of religious liberty guaranteed in the First Amendment, the individual should have the right to determine what he takes to be the meaning of religion. If the individual does not have this right, then governmental protection of religious liberty turns out to be illusory, for the government could simply classify an individual's religion as a nonreligious, secular sort of thing and proceed to regulate it outside the protection of the First Amendment. On the other hand, the First Amendment prohibits to the government an establishment of religion. How can the government act on this injunction unless it can determine what is and what is not *a religion*? I believe that the public schools are not entirely free from this kind of dilemma, although the context within which the difficulty is to be confronted is not necessarily a legal one.

One may also look at the problem of what the term "religion" means in the context of a policy directive relative to teaching about religion. Religion can be seen as having various facets or dimensions, such as the following:

1. Religion as a body of dogma—the creedal side of religion.
2. Religion as the structure, organization, and activities of a church: the ecclesiastical side of religion.
3. Religion as a social institution, fulfilling certain social functions in interaction with other social institutions.

4. Religion as the intellectual organization of basic questions and their alternative answers—the theological dimension.
5. Religion as an aspect of social conflict and adjustment—an aspect of the sociology of intergroup relations.
6. Religion as a state of exaltation undergone by the individual: the ascetic, the mystical, the personalistic aspect of religion.

This is certainly not an exhaustive list, but it is suggestive of the many different angles from which the study of religion might be approached. In all probability not all of these would be included with equal ease in a school program where the intent is to teach *about* religion. Critical analysis and selection would therefore have to be made.

Objectivity and Neutrality

Almost invariably when proposals are made that the public schools should teach about religion, it is asserted that of course this should be done impartially, objectively, or neutrally. These terms may not be synonymous, but it must be granted that they all raise some kind of problem. It sometimes appears that those individuals who most vehemently urge upon us a policy of teaching about religion assume that the problem, such as it may be, is resolved by the simple proposal to teach about religion. The problem, I am convinced, is not that simple, and it is *un*-simple in at least two ways. As frail human beings we often fail to act as we, in our ideal conception of ourselves, know we ought to act. Moreover, the problem is complicated by the fact that the ideal itself is unclear. That is, it is not only that objectivity (neutrality, etc.) is hard for us poor frail humans to achieve: we are not at all sure (collectively, at least) just what objectivity requires within this setting. The words of William B. Ball, Counsel to the National Catholic Education Association, are illuminating at this point:

> It may perhaps be perceived that for a Catholic teacher in a public school to "teach about" the origins of the Established Church in England might be no simple feat—or, if simple, perhaps dubiously successful. Or consider the agnostic teacher who "taught about" the Catholic doctrine of Transubstantiation. Of course, the matter of value expressions would reach into many areas other than the more obviously religious. The moral crises of history—the moral monstrosities in history—how should they be described? In the history of the Jews, the persecutions under Hitler would be encountered. Should no value judgments be expressed? How would one "teach about" the experience of the Jewish people under Heydrich? More precisely, would moral judgments be made, and if so, according to what standard, what ultimate principle? But the rendering of the judgment takes us at once from the realm of "teaching about" into the realm of "teaching of" and squarely confronts the central problem of official orthodoxies.[2]

With due recognition of the intellectual tangles involved in the deep-rooted character of the problem of objectivity in education, two quite different meanings may be identified. If objectivity means the putting aside of one's values, being partisan to nothing in the controversy, it is to be feared that there is no resolution of the difficulty, for the reason that such an aim is impossible to pursue. Such attempts inevitably wind up with a freight of covert values being unwittingly smuggled in. It is a delusion to think that a value-loaded problem can be handled in a completely *valueless* way. Another meaning to objectivity, however, is not encumbered with the same kinds of difficulties; this is a conception of objectivity along the lines of openness and fullness in revealing one's own point of view, combined with fairness and adequacy in reporting the views of others. An essential aspect of this view of objectivity, thus, would be to render clear and unmistakable to others the various foundation stones and building blocks of one's analysis. This is difficult but it has the merit of not needing to be carried out to the point of perfection in order to achieve useful results.

Public and Private Knowledge

To teach about religion is presumably to ask youngsters to acquire knowledge about religion. It is appropriate to ask here whether this knowledge is to be "public knowledge" or "private knowledge." Recognizing that some people would raise serious question as to whether knowledge can ever be private and non-public, let us use the terms here as if the distinction were a valid one. Public knowledge involves what can be communicated to others in such a publicly identifiable way that it can be checked out—verified. It involves a publicly agreed-upon set of conceptual categories, a conventional language to represent these concepts, and sufficient empirical rooting for the concepts and terms so that inter-observer agreement is possible. There is, on the other hand, a kind of knowing centering in our apprehensions of our own private consciousness, but this kind of knowing defies the sort of clear communication which enables others to judge the meaning and validity of such private experiences. Let us call this type of knowing private knowledge, and recognize that by its very nature, insofar as it is *private*, it is not publicly verifiable. Various art forms such as poetry deal with this dimension of our experience, but there is no way to know whether the response evoked by a poem in one reader is similar to what is evoked in another reader, or whether either of these is similar to the experience upon which the poem may have been built.

When someone asserts that he has had a vision of God or of an angel and that he has been authoritatively commanded to do this or that, perhaps even to give a set of moral imperatives to the rest of us, there is no way that another person can ascertain on reliable grounds whether it did or did not happen in the way asserted, or, if it did, what it might mean. We cannot reasonably deny that a person has had the kind of private experience he asserts he has had. But, on the other hand, neither is there any reliable way for us to use such testimony as our own knowledge. Nor is it a question of attacking the honesty of the other person who claims such private knowledge. There is a vast difference between reporting accurately the state of one's conscious mind and being able to assert that the content of that state of mind has any definite meaning for the nonmental world. Hallucinations, for instance, are real states of mind, but their content is not necessarily representative of any truth about the nonmental world. Similarly, when someone reports that he has had a revelation or an intuition, we do not know what to do with such a report. What is its meaning for the realm of existence beyond the experiencing mind? Unless we can get some anchor points in the experience of others, private experience is doomed—not necessarily to be untrue or unreal, but to be unusable on a reliable basis by others. It cannot become publicly available. The difficulty shows up most sharply when two contradictory formulations of private experience confront each other. How to adjudicate between them? There appear to be no rules to decide which is valid.

The basis of the world's traditional religions is in the realm of private knowledge: direct revelation, mystic experience, and that ineffable form of knowledge known as intuition. It is not merely that different religions give different and contradictory answers on many important matters, with no way that has ever been demonstrated to judge between the various claims. But further, what a large group of people agree on does not in itself have any reliable claim to truth or validity. One hundred million Buddhists believing in the efficacy of their prayer wheels does not give credibility to statements that prayer wheels will have the effect attributed to them. That is, private knowledge does not become public knowledge no matter what number of individuals allegedly have the same private experience. Numerical consensus has nothing to do with the rules for establishing a proposition as true.

The distinction between public and private knowledge as applied to religion becomes sharper when we remember that the imperatives of religions, the "shalts" and "shalt nots," the definitions of sin (indeed the very conception of sin) are derived from the realm of nonpublic knowledge. These imperatives are accepted as binding not only upon the individual having the private experience, but it is asserted that others also— perhaps mankind in general—should follow suit.

The distinction that I have drawn between public and private knowledge can be related to the problem of this essay in the following question: If the public school is to provide knowledge about religion, is that knowledge to be the publicly communicable and testable variety or is it to be the kind of knowledge accessible only to the mind and consciousness of individuals and locked away from public scrutiny? This is a fundamental question for the public schools to decide. Furthermore, there is a second-order question that must be dealt with. Shall the very distinction between public and private knowledge be made available to students as an intellectual tool and resource for working with the problems of the factual dimensions of religion?

Closely connected with the issue of private and public knowledge is the problem of secondhand knowledge. In a complex and highly specialized society such as ours, the basic sources of our existence are often obscure and remote. What we learn at many points is secondhand and difficult to fit into our picture of more directly experienced situations. Even if all that is offered as knowledge were true and valid, there would still be the enormous problem of its *meaning* to a given individual. By its very nature the school must present much of its learning in a context remote from the settings in which the meaning can be most clearly apprehended. Motivating students to learn may sometimes drive a teacher to distraction, and this problem of motivation is tied up with the meaninglessness of material abstracted from any life context that the student can recognize and accept. Even in the most rigorous fields of natural science, where confidence in the self-corrective methods of science can be engendered, there are serious problems of learning what someone else (the scientist) knows but which in a real sense is not yet *known* by the student. If it is true that much of the learning that goes on even in science classes is of the sort that might be expressed as "learning words which represent what someone else is said to know," how much more likely is this to be true when students are asked to learn about religion—where much of the knowledge is not only secondhand (third-hand, 1000th-hand), but *private* knowledge as well.

The Error of Quaintness

There is a way of teaching about other peoples and their cultures which has already achieved a foothold in the elementary schools of our country. I call it the error of quaintness. To designate something as interesting from a quaint point of view is to make a patronizing judgment from a position of assumed superiority. The quaint custom or mode of dress is not something which the speaker considers seriously for himself; for the speaker who perceives something as quaint there is no deep involvement or significance. It is probably no accident that dolls—unhuman images of humans—are sometimes referred to as

quaint. Are not Eskimos and American Indians often approached in elementary school as people with quaint ways?
Such ways presumably could never be our ways nor, insofar
as they are seen as quaint, could they be the basis for any
consequential learning on our part. Most film travelogues are
the very essence of the quaint approach: essentially a dehuman-
ized if not always inhuman mode of dealing with people and
their cultures. As one reads about the introduction of Hanukkah
celebrations into schools with predominantly non-Jewish student bodies, the impression is that this often is done with a
patronizing approach of quaintness. If the experiencing of ceremonies of another's religion does not throw light upon the
very nature of the language of symbols and enlarge one's whole
appreciation of this dimension of man and his nature as he
attempts to express deep feelings in symbolic terms, perhaps
there is nothing very educative about it and there is a real
question as to its place in our schools.

Sometimes in the heat of controversy over the inclusion of
religion in the public school program there is perhaps too much
attention to avoiding offense and to soothing ruffled feelings of
righteous indignation and too little attention to what will contribute substantially to the genuine educative growth of youngsters. Have not the public schools often in the past, in the name
of what seems to be a rather simple-minded piety, given implicit
approval, as in certain released-time programs, to rigidly memo-
riter, rote-learning activity that has no justification in *any*
theory of educative growth?

The Bible as Literature

Statements urging that the public schools teach about religion
commonly include strong approval of using the Bible in the

schools, if it is to be studied as literature. Since it is generally agreed that parts of the Bible are indeed of high literary merit, presumably there is no problem here.

But perhaps it is not so simple as this. Besides the problem of selecting the parts of the Bible that not only deserve literary attention but also may be regarded as suitable for discussion with adolescents, there is the question of using the regular tools of literary analysis and study. The study of literature on any serious basis is much more than a process of reading off the written word and being transported with appreciative delight! The identification and analysis of metaphor, myth, symbol, and allegory is part of the stock-in-trade of the student of literature. Is there not a problem as to what parts of the Bible are literal truth and what parts metaphor or allegory? Could we agree objectively on the metaphorical status of the Book of Genesis narrative of creation and of the events of the Garden of Eden? Are the American people ready to let high-school youth study the Bible as literature, in terms of myth and symbol, metaphor and allegory? Are school people prepared to defend genuine educative approaches? Shall the class in literature skip over the 16th chapter of Saint Matthew, 18th verse, where in the King James version, it says, "That thou art Peter, and upon this rock I will build my church"? Or, shall this be opened up as a question of allegory or literal truth? Is the Song of Solomon a beautiful poem about the love of a somewhat tarnished but definitely human woman, or is it an allegory of the love between Christ and his ever imperfect Church? It is to be feared that generally those parts of the Bible which are most likely to be considered of high literary value are precisely those parts which are replete with myth, allegory, metaphor, and symbol.

This line of inquiry may be carried a little farther in a slightly different direction. Is the Bible the only piece of sacred literature that should find its way into the school program as an object of literary study? Is the Koran to be included? The Torah? Any Buddhist literature? The Book of Mormon? If the Bible is the only sacred literature to be included, can the assertion that its inclusion is *for literary purposes only* really be the true one? To move in still another direction, what is the probability of getting students and teachers to approach the Bible in any reasonably objective fashion in most American communities, where the critical probings that are a standard part of literary analysis are very much apt to be denounced in the community as sacrilegious? That fears along this line are not entirely groundless is evidenced in the urging by national church bodies that Bibles courses in private religious institutions be given public high school credit.

Religiosity and Religious Conformity

It is a commonplace fact that our age places an unusually high value upon outward and superficial appearances of piety; at least, such appearances are condemned by a large number of clerical leaders in the various major faiths. Church attendance is at an all-time high; we are offered religion as the road to peace of mind; and feelings of self-righteousness come easily through the denunciation of atheists, godless Communism, and the like. In this atmosphere of religious togetherness many people find nothing disturbing about the local advertising councils enhancing their public image by paying for space in the advertising media to urge people to go to the church of their choice. It apparently does not make any difference to which church one goes; membership in any conventional religious organization will bring respectability and acceptability. It seems to make no difference that some religions give thorough and basic support to the free, inquiring mind while others operate within a rigid context of authoritarian dogmatism. Apparently the *kind* of religion does not matter, only that it can be called religion by some conventional set of criteria, usually linked with ortho-dox forms of Western theism.

One may not expect much depth or integrity from institu-tions whose driving motive is sales and profits, but one feels that an educational institution has an obligation to approach such matters from a somewhat deeper and more thoughtful point of view. In another part of the Educational Policies Com-mission's book, *Moral and Spiritual Values in the Public Schools*, there are statements which are easily interpreted as expressing a kind of religious conformity not too different from that revealed by the full-page ads, the billboards, and the rear ends of taxicabs urging us all indiscriminately to go to church:

> The attitude of the public schools toward the various religious beliefs of the children in their care should be one of friendly and sympathetic understanding. This attitude can be revealed without in any way compromising the personal religious con-victions of the teachers and without giving the endorsement of the public schools to any religious faith. The words and the attitude of the teacher should be such as to reassure each child that his religious beliefs are considered to be right *for him*, so that he will feel comfortable with his own creed or lack of creed.

> The school that enrolls children who attend several different churches should capitalize on the educational opportunity which this diversity offers. . . . Respect for the individual right of each child will require the teacher to assume and, moreover, actually to *feel* an attitude of respect and reverence for these faiths and observances.[3]

This passage is asserting a generally conformist position. No matter what religion a child has, *it is right for him!* Teachers are actually to *feel* reverence for any and all religions! Now, no responsible teacher would sanction direct attacks upon the religious beliefs or practices of a young child by a teacher. The child has no resources to defend himself against this sort of thing. But to restrain from deliberately inhumane attacks upon a vulnerable child is quite a different thing from the notion of approving the religion as good for the child. It is also a far cry from feeling reverence for a religion which may deserve on the whole little more than abhorrence. It seems beyond the conception of some writers in this field that some religions may be bad or have demonstrably bad features. If a child holds to a religion that asserts that all modern science is a delusion of the secularists, should the teacher in her "reverence" for "what is right for the child" make sure that he learns nothing of modern science, which might well undermine his religious views? It is quite possible that in the interests of prudence and practicality we may not be able to help public school children acquire the tools for critical discrimination between better and worse forms of religion, as we would want to do in art or any other comparable field. But let us admit, if this is the case, that what we are doing is not really best for the child, but that it is one of those unlovely compromises with reality that the schools, as creatures of a sometimes indifferent and not always wise public, must from time to time make.

Let us look a little further in the same document. The next paragraph is:

> The avowed atheist and the opinionated bigot may alike object to even the most objective presentation of the facts about the role of religion in American life. Such views can not be allowed to cripple this important aspect of American public education. Even though a few children may come from the homes of Communist or other totalitarian opinion, the public schools teach the principles of democracy. So too the public schools should teach all children a decent respect for the re-

ligious opinions of mankind and the basic culture of mankind. Teachers should not hesitate to show that they approve of participation in religious activities on the part of their pupils.[4]

The first sentence of this passage contains a real rabbit punch! Not only is "atheist" connected with "the opinionated bigot" by juxtaposition in the sentence, but apparently the *theist* is capable of an objectivity that lies beyond the *atheist*. What is the significance of speaking of children from Communist homes in the sentence in close proximity to the sentence referring to atheists? Any doubt as to the essential conformist message of the passage is dispelled by the last sentence: "Teachers should not hesitate to show that they approve of participation in religious activities on the part of their pupils."

Today the forces of conformity in religion raise doubts as to how inclusive a public school program is likely to be in teaching about religion. Remembering that it took the Supreme Court of the United States to prevent the state of Maryland from barring a notary public from his position on the ground that he did not believe in God, and remembering that atheism and agnosticism have been widely identified in the popular mind with Communism, we may have some grounds for fear over the kind of mandate for teaching about religion to be given the public schools. Such teaching may in many cases tend to be an aid and comfort to conventional piety and to the forces of religious conformity of our time. As we have noted, the power to define what religion means is the power under some circumstances to say which claims shall be dismissed from attention. There are those who feel that teaching about religion should include only the beliefs of conventionally recognized and organized religious bodies. The history of civil liberty in the United States seems to have made it abundantly clear that freedom of religion is virtually meaningless unless it includes freedom to deny, criticize, or ignore what commonly goes under the name of religion. Hence, to teach about religion must, for genuine educative purposes, include negative as well as positive perspectives on religion.

Will public schools, many of which include prayers and Bible reading in direct defiance of the Supreme Court, give the same kind of attention to various forms of ethical naturalism, anthropocentric humanism, atheism, and other nontheisms as they do to more conventional points of view? Will they afford any real insight into the claims of religious existentialism, for instance, most forms of which seem to attack all religions as man-made obstacles to a valid relation between man and God? Has the public school shown signs yet of being able to help young people understand the point of view of the committed pacifist, who almost always reaches his pacifism by a road that in some meaningful sense must be called religious?

Religion in History and Religion as a View of History

It is generally agreed that the teaching of Western history without reference to religion would be a badly truncated approach to historical study. The Diaspora of the Jews, the Christianization of the Roman Empire, the Middle Ages as essentially a Christian Catholic civilization, the medieval pogroms, the Protestant Reformation, the American Puritan experience in our colonial period, to name just a few, are examples of events and movements in history that could hardly be justifiably omitted. In addition to ordinary problems of objectivity in the teaching and study of religious events and movements in history, there is another problem, associated with the often recurring phrase "the role which religion has played in history." Recall that this phrase appeared twice in the passages quoted above from the Educational Policies Commission statement.

Public schools are urged by many to make sure that our young people learn *about* this role played by religion. The word "role" in this context seems never to be used in the plural; it is always "the role." What people seem to have in mind is a set of fairly definite one-sided effects produced by religion, and these effects are on the whole favorable, even though occasionally someone reminds us that there are some rather ugly episodes in the history of religion. These writers do not seem to be simply calling for the identification and honest assessment of causes and effects where they may be reliably established. The contest seems rather to suggest an a priori judgment, a form of special pleading in which the results are known and prejudged in advance of inquiry.

"The role of religion in history," proposed as an imperative for inclusion in the public school program, is as difficult to deal with in the scholarly study of the historical past as the topics of "the role of government in history" or "the role of art in history." It is quite possible here that a Trojan horse marked "teaching *about* religion" has been offered the public schools. Should it be drawn within the walls, however, the hidden soldiers would perhaps later be found fighting on the side of "teaching *of* religion."

Religion may be studied in connection with history not merely as one class of events to be taken into account as part of the general study of history. Most religions are, or contain within themselves, a view of history: a general logic of the human scene by which the significance of events can be interpreted. Human life is seen as having a Purpose as part of the Cosmic Script. A simplistic caricature of the orthodox Christian view of history serves as an illustration: history in such terms is a drama with the first act set in the Garden of Eden. It is a story of a Fall and a Redemption. The actors' parts are already set and the general tenor of their lines decided. They may ad lib only within set limits. Does one simply tell students, as a digressive observation, that the Christian view of history is such-and-such, within a course organized in terms of another, perhaps secular, view of history? Or should the course in the history of Western civilization be organized on the basis of some *one* Christian (or Jewish or whatever) view of history, with passing mention that there are other possible ways to select, organize, and interpret the materials of history? Whatever the answer may be, it would seem that the phrase "to teach about" has lost another portion of its initial simplicity and clarity.

It can be seen that the difficulties which a school will in all likelihood encounter as it attempts to translate the general policy position of teaching about religion into concrete terms are not merely difficulties posed by obstreperous groups within the community. Most of the problems discussed in this essay contain such basic unresolved elements as how a democratic people deals with matters which are not fully open to scrutiny and discussion and for which the principle of majority rule seems to be less than fully adequate. In effect, what has been said in this essay is, "Let us by all means teach about religion in the public schools, but there are some very poor ways to do this. Let us try to identify these and avoid them wherever possible." In seeking a more permanent solution to the problem of the place of religion in public education, it is to be hoped that the issue will soon be considered with less attention to keeping community groups quiet and more to what is educationally defensible in a society of and for free men.

Chapter Ten

•

WHAT CHURCHES SHOULD
EXPECT OF PUBLIC SCHOOLS

DEAN M. KELLEY

The public schools serve the churches and the synagogues best when they do their own work well, rather than trying to do the work of churches.

We are fortunate that recent Supreme Court decisions on prayers and Bible reading in public schools have made the topic of religion in the schools one of common knowledge. We are less fortunate, perhaps, that the same events have precipitated some rather dogmatic views on the subject in many minds. But it is interesting to note that the views of many have changed or broadened since the first such decision.

For five years, the Reverend Dean M. Kelley has served as Executive Director of Religious Liberty with the National Council of Churches of Christ in the U.S.A. He coordinated the National Study Conference on Church and State in Columbus, Ohio. Following this conference, he spoke to a conference of public school teachers at Indiana University, and this presentation serves as the basis of this chapter. He is the author of "Protestants and Parochial Schools" in a special issue of *Commonweal*, published by Helicon Press in 1964.

The Real Issue

The real issue hangs on what we expect of our public schools. I suggest that church people have been expecting too much of them, and in the case of religious practices, they have been expecting the wrong things. They have been acting as though the churches and the nation were in deadly peril if children did not say their prayers daily in the public school classroom! Is it really such a life-and-death issue to the churches, to religion, to the nation, whether these routine, ritual practices continue? Is this something they should fight and die for, for the sake of Holy Faith?

Historically, these casual, perfunctory, state-sponsored forms of religion have not made a great deal of difference in determining morality or character. Certainly the public schools of Imperial and Weimar Germany had ample devotional rituals, and children were instructed in their catechisms regularly by public school teachers. But this did not prevent the rise of Hitler or the slaughter of the Jews. It did not produce righteousness or even a reverence that made any difference in human conduct. It never has and it never will. It is not on this level that religion changes lives.

Let us try to distinguish one level of religion from another. We could rank religions along a line from those which make a high or even total demand upon their members to those which make little or no demand. At which end of this continuum would you find the religious movements *that make a difference?* Where would the disciples of Jesus be? ("He who does not renounce all that he has cannot be my disciple." Luke 14:33.)

Where would the monastic orders stand in this sequence, with their vows of poverty, chastity, and obedience? Where would the first Reform movements be, in which men risked their possessions, families, and lives for their faith? Where would the French Huguenots be found? The early Methodists? The Pilgrims? The Mormons? The Jehovah's Witnesses? These little bands of dedicated men and women have cut through the dessicated crust of a stagnant society like a buzz-saw through peanut brittle.

There is wisdom in the principle that religious movements will achieve effects in direct proportion to the demands they make of their adherents. The less effort, the less effect. And the chief vice of religious practices in public schools is not merely that they are unjust to nonbelievers (which they are), but that they are ineffective for believers and tend to dilute and weaken the significance of religion for them. Routine and casual and collective recitations of religious material in public schools is a form of least-effort, low-demand religion that falls near the bottom of the line of possible manifestations of religion. It is probably about the easiest, cheapest kind of religion one can imagine, short of a prayer wheel. What costs little accomplishes little, in religion as anywhere else.

Meaningless Practices

In addition to being religiously ineffective, recitations of devotional material can be harmful to the religious development of some persons, though not necessarily to all. If one thinks of high-demand religion (certainly historic Christianity and historic Judaism), it is something that has set men on fire with zeal and devotion across the ages. This fever is contagious when communicated at full strength from person to person. But if a person is exposed to it in attenuated form or inoculated with the dead virus from which all the glow and sparkle has faded, his resistance to the real thing may be increased until he becomes immune to the demand of a religion that would make a difference in his life. "Oh, I know all about that stuff," he might think. "We had all that in school, along with spelling and the multiplication table, and I'm tired of it all. Now that I don't have to go to school any more, I don't have to go along with the religion business either."

What I am trying to suggest is that, far from being an essential of survival for the Christian or other churches, least-common-denominator devotional recitations of religion-in-general in public schools may actually work against the survival of the kind of Christianity that counts—by deceiving Christians into the notion that they are being very religious because children pray in the schools. The churches have little to gain and much to lose from devotional practices in public schools, and churches are gradually beginning to discover this. Synagogues, on the other hand, seem to know it already, for they have not been pressuring public schools to do the work of religious institutions. Quite the contrary, they know that religious faith is virtually indestructible, for they have survived at least fifteen centuries of systematic persecution at the hands of "Christians."

Wide Range . . . Responsibilities and Means

Religious groups have been only one of many community forces pressuring the public schools to supply every deficiency and remedy every ill in our common life together. Thus, public schools are striving to teach everything from basket-weaving to basketball, including sex education, driver education, and—apparently—religious education. And they are being asked to do all this on inadequate resources of time and money, to teach more and more with less and less!

The results have been several, all bad. Education has gotten thinner and flatter as it has been stretched to cover more territory. In addition, public educators have conceived the understandable notion that they are responsible for all the education of all the children, a potentially totalitarian delusion of the first order. But why should they think otherwise when all other institutions of the community have seemingly been willing to unload their responsibilities upon the tax-supported common schools? ("Let the public schools do it; isn't that what we pay taxes for?") There might be some excuse for messianic pretensions among public school educators if they were turning out graduates of educational excellence. But they are not consistently doing so.

It is not reasonable to be an advocate of "basic education" or any other kind of educational fundamentalism which wants to limit public schools to "reading, writing, and arithmetic" as taught in McGuffey Readers. I do wish the average graduates of the average high school could spell, but spelling is not one of the higher skills, and Shakespeare was not distinguished for his consistency in spelling, even his own name. Algebra, too, has been overrated as a skill necessary for every citizen of the nation. I know a number of able, conscientious, and "successful" citizens who don't know anything about algebra and don't need to. But I must admit it would be helpful if high school graduates could read well, rapidly, and with a high degree of comprehension, and could translate reading material into meaning, action, and decision. A citizen who can't read, and I mean read effectively, is not fully a participating citizen.

The point is that the prime task of the public schools is to teach those subjects we most nearly agree are essential to our common life in this nation. That means both the tool-skills of the three R's and the rudiments of our cultural heritage (history, literature, government, art, music, science). After an unquestionable level of excellence has been achieved in teaching these subjects to students, *then* the public schools might use whatever time and resources remain for teaching additional courses.

Education, National Survival, and Tradition

Public education is one of the really essential means of survival to our society; if it fails in its task of preparing our children to function capably and effectively as citizens, our way of life will be in jeopardy. Therefore, I should like to see the public schools given much more of our national resources than we are able to give on a local property-based level of taxation and to see them stripped for action, discarding all that can be done by others and doing all that others cannot do. Thereby, they would truly earn the respect and gratitude of everyone, including the churches and synagogues.

Children cannot read the Scriptures if they cannot read. Is it nothing to the churches that the public schools prepare children to read the Holy Scriptures, as well as other materials? Children cannot understand the mighty acts of God in history if they do not know history. Is it nothing to the churches that the public schools teach history?

Perhaps an example will make this clearer. I used to teach a confirmation course for junior-high youngsters which lasted a year. During that year, I was accustomed to having virtually one hundred per cent attendance—on Saturday morning—because the class was something important, serious, exciting, and systematic. The youngsters did their homework regularly and in other ways met the rather high demands I made of them because this was something they wanted to do, enjoyed doing, would rather do than stay at home or wander around the streets. We do not need to rely on the coercive power of the state to make young people learn about religion; all we need to do is let the glory shine through and treat religion with the excitement and urgency and respect we say it merits, rather than dampen and dull it into the same category as spelling and algebra.

It was soon obvious that if I wanted to teach those boys and girls anything about the Reformers or the Crusades or the Roman Empire, I virtually had to start from the beginning, because they did not have much notion of what happened in the fascinating, tragic, and heroic history of the human race, let alone whether Martin Luther or John Wesley came first, or before or after Charlemagne!

At that time, I would very happily have traded several hours' worth of Regents' Prayers for a little more solid preparation in world history. The public schools would have served my religious concerns best by providing an adequate foundation in "secular" history upon which a minister could build some structure of religious development.

This need is not met by the pietism of a certain fourth-grade history text, which treats the Egyptians and the Greeks in good scholarly fashion and then inserts between them a chapter on the Hebrews taken almost literally from the Book of Chronicles, a tactic which is neither good history nor good religion. Rather than teach a little mediocre religion at the behest of misguided churchmen, the public schools should concentrate on teaching good, reliable history, and teaching it well, and leave the religious interpretation to the churches and synagogues.

Now, one must *not* say that religion should be omitted from history or any other subject. In fact, that is where we have gone most seriously astray in our expectations of the public schools. We have felt that the public schools have some responsibility toward religion, but we have assumed it was devotional—having the children sing hymns and pray and read the Bible without comment.

More and more people are realizing that the public schools *do* have a responsibility toward religion but that it is instructional, not devotional. Not only is it a duty to teach "secular" subjects well—a major service to the churches and to everyone else—but it is a duty to include in that "secular" instruction the important role that religion has played in shaping our history, our literature, our social institutions, our art and music. This does not mean indoctrination or teaching for commitment. The public school teacher of history who is effective in his profession, for instance, does not care whether his pupils are Christian, Jewish, or nonreligious, but he does want them to understand what happened in history as well as they are able at their particular level of maturity: why the Reformation came about and what its effects were up to our day; the role of the Christian movement in the Roman Empire, before and after Constantine; the failures of religion in Czarist Russia and its consequent denunciation and exploitation by the Soviets; etc. There are some ugly episodes in the history of all religions, but it is useless to try to cover them up; rather we should try to understand them and prevent their recurrence. A public school graduate who does not have some notion of this dimension of our common heritage is inadequately educated for today's world.

Can this really be done objectively? If churchmen would leave the public schools alone, educational progress could be made. To be sure, the few poor or lazy teachers would not achieve much for history or religion however they tried to present them, but a teacher who likes his subject and wants to confront his pupils with its fascinations can only welcome the added interest that the religious aspect gives, provided a flurry of complaints and counter-complaints is not stirred every time religion is mentioned.

Objective, Skillful, and Cooperative

The churches should expect from public schools, and should get, no special favors. In general subject matter religion should be treated with the same scholarly objectivity as politics, literature, science, and mathematics. I purposely include politics to remind us that religion is not the only subject on which parents and others are touchy. A good public school tries to treat all subjects fairly, objectively, giving the range of interpretations where authorities are not agreed. To avoid religious or political controversy by simply eliminating both topics from classroom instruction is to emasculate education and to establish a sectarian concept of life that no one should want. People will always disagree strongly on those religious and political matters for which they hold passionate beliefs, but they should desire for their children a fullness and fairness of treatment, which should be the hallmark of public schools, rather than a pale timidity or an aggressive humanism.

The public school is not the sole agent of education. Each man in his life receives many educations, from many sources, with many different interpretations of man and reality. One of the most essential parts of education is to learn to weigh and compare one interpretation with another to distinguish truth from falsehood. Beware of the totalitarian tendency of some educators to try to fit every form of education into the One Great Integrated Curriculum: that way lies the rule of mindless conformity. We must learn to test the claims of political parties, commercial advertisers, and churches. Public schools, churches, and all other educational institutions serve as healthy correctives to one another's propaganda and pretensions. We should be thankful that they do, for the public schools serve the cause of truth when they enable us to distinguish it from falsehood, wherever either may be found.

Chapter Eleven

•

ADMINISTRATIVE ASPECTS
OF SHARED-TIME PROGRAMS

MELVIN P. HELLER

Parochial schools have come in for a certain amount of criticism on the ground that they tend to divide society, while even those who defend the right of parents to educate their children in their own faith concede that the financial problems of church-related schools are becoming increasingly severe. The numerous proposals for solving the parochial school dilemma range from total elimination of church-supported schools to increased federal aid to these schools. Recently compromise plans have been suggested whereby public and parochial schools engage in a cooperative endeavor which requires them to share time, staff, and/or facilities. Such shared-time plans have been implemented in large and in small cities, especially in the states of Michigan, Ohio, and Pennsylvania.

Dr. Melvin P. Heller, an Associate Professor at Loyola University in Chicago, served the Educational Research Council of Greater Cleveland and the Ridgewood High School, Norridge, Illinois, before returning to his alma mater. In 1962 he was a John Hay Fellow at Colorado College.

Because of the 1965 legislation granting some types of federal aid to education (see Chapter Four), many educators feel that the implications are strong for a significant increase in shared-time experiments in all sections of the country.

This chapter will consider those aspects of shared time which might be of concern to administrators. The problems are examined through a series of questions which reflect the following considerations: (1) curriculum, (2) faculty, (3) scheduling, (4) allegiance of pupils, (5) extracurricular and athletic programs, (6) community reaction, (7) pupil accountability, (8) finance, and (9) facilities.

Obviously, cooperation among public and parochial school personnel is the key to the successful implementation of shared-time programs. Grades can be circulated between the cooperating schools, and either the public or the parochial school can accept the responsibility for the determination of grade-point averages, class ranking, and the like. Schedules and school rules can be worked out to accommodate the pupils and the teachers who are involved in the sharing of facilities.

The mingling of public and parochial school pupils can have many distinct social and cultural advantages, but before plunging into the deep waters in which the concept of shared time is immersed, administrators, school boards, and patrons are obliged to think through some of the implications of the problems involved.

The questions raised here are typical of those questions which must be answered by administrators if shared-time programs are to work. The success or failure of present practices can be important as guides, but the treatment in this chapter is intended to elaborate the concept of shared-time programs and to aid in situations where shared-time practices are either in effect or contemplated for the future.

What Are the Implications of "Secular" and "Religious" Subjects?

Public school administrators and school board members seldom receive clear-cut directions from the many philosophies in our pluralistic society unless they accept a monolithic framework. This paradox is what the public and parochial school officials must face if they are to decide upon which subjects should be taught under whose jurisdiction in a shared-time plan. In general practice the subjects classified as secular are mathematics, science, foreign languages, physical education, and vocational education. Those generally classified as parochial are social studies, English, fine arts, and religion. Even if the ambiguity of these divisions were not immediately obvious, there are other problems implicit in this classification of subjects. What is to prevent the teachers of any subject from demonstrating and teaching their own atttitudes and biases in their treatment of what they teach? What is the difference between literature in a foreign language and literature in English as a vehicle for the expression of values? It is almost impossible to exclude a teacher's philosophical, religious, and moral values inherent in and applied to the subject which he teaches. Moreover, in the interest of an enriched, correlated approach to the curriculum a teacher of a secular subject is likely to ignore the artificial barrier of subject division and "encroach" upon a "parochial" subject.

The hierarchy of subjects must also be considered. The usual division of courses gives the public schools academic control over math and sciences and provides for parochial control over the humanities, except for foreign languages. A question may arise concerning the attitude of a student toward these subjects and toward those who teach them. The student may not agree with nor understand the criteria which determined the division; but if he identifies himself primarily with one school, he may erroneously consider subjects taught in the other school as devoid of values, and therefore not worth serious study. It seems that an integrated approach to learning is tacitly undermined when the "value" subjects are taught by one group and the "practical" subjects are taught by another. The ability of public and parochial instructional leaders will be tested to the maximum if strength can result from this division of the curriculum through the creation of artificial barriers.

What Is to be Done with Displaced Teachers from Parochial Schools?

Once the question of division of subjects into secular and religious has been decided for a given community, the question arises of what to do with the parochial school teachers whose subjects have been designated as under secular jurisdiction. Assuming that mathematics would be classified as a "public school" subject, what is to become of the priest or nun whose academic major and teaching skill is in mathematics? To suggest that this person develop another major or find another outlet is unrealistic. Although the displaced members of religious orders might be transferred to localities where the shared-time concept is not in effect, such a transfer would merely postpone the necessity to face squarely how to make the best use of competent teachers.

Perhaps the question can be answered in terms of staff utilization rather than in terms of secular and religious subjects. The teachers of mathematics, for example, whether public or parochial, can work as a team so that the talents of all can be extended to the students. Another way to use the talents of the "displaced" teachers would be to encourage them to do research in their subject areas and to share their findings with those who have been designated to teach those subjects. Administrative encouragement must be made evident in terms of time, facilities, finances, and opportunities. Implementation of this suggestion requires a degree of cooperation among administrators and teachers which is not common. Yet the very force of the necessity to cooperate for the purpose of improved education may be the major breakthrough in the whole problem of religion and the public schools.

What Schedule Modifications Are Necessary?

Obviously a pupil's schedule must allow sufficient time for him to leave one building and to arrive on time for classes in another. The schedule must be flexible enough to provide for this leeway without causing those who are in the receiving building to idle away their time waiting for the arrival of additional students. Modular scheduling with several sections of a course overlapping in time may solve this problem with or without major changes in the program of the public school students. Even though many difficulties are involved in developing a satisfactory modular, overlapping schedule, they are of little importance when compared to the alternative of officially encouraged, daily time-wasting.

Another problem relevant to scheduling is adequate sections of those public school courses which will have heavy enrollments from the parochial school and fewer sections for those which will have only a few parochial enrollees. To compound the problem, the decision concerning the number of parochial students in public school courses seems to rest with parochial officials. Obviously, time, space, and personnel factors have to be coordinated between the receiving and the sending schools.

If several schools are involved, this coordination becomes increasingly more complex.

It appears evident that rigid, conventional scheduling is inadequate in light of these considerations. Perhaps flexible scheduling and/or the extension of the school day or week can provide workable answers.

What Happens to the "Whole Child" Concept?

It is very possible that the division of subjects, staff, and facilities into secular and parochial categories can actually highlight differences in the very aspects of a child's education which shared-time plans are devised to equalize. Separation of subjects may have ramifications similar to those which were decried in the famous desegregation decisions. Whether fact or fancy, a stigma may be attached to each group by members of the other group. It is possible that the classification of students, a necessity for administrative coordination, could emphasize certain real as well as artificial differences which exist among the students, their homes, and their teachers. The result of the emphasis could confuse the child to the degree that the potential benefits of shared-time plans would be weakened. Social, emotional, and intellectual acceptance and adjustment on the part of parochial and public school students and teachers are topics worth the consideration of administrators.

What Happens to Pupil Allegiances?

Psychologists have much to say about the need for people to belong to a group. Since shared-time practices require that a student attend part-time at two schools, there is a danger that he may wonder where he belongs. If this danger becomes a reality, not only psychological problems but also administrative problems can develop. The divided allegiances of a student may have a deleterious effect upon such factors as school morale, participation in activities, classroom discipline, dropout decisions, college plans, and curricular provisions. For instance, in a discipline case, which school should do the reprimanding? Will the parochial student who "acts up" in the public school cast a poor reflection upon "his" school? Will the parochial school where he "belongs" punish him, too?

The question of allegiances and divided loyalties comes into focus in relation to extracurricular and intraschool activities. Separate activities and teams for public and for parochial schools may keep loyalties intact, but this separateness may have a negative effect upon student acceptance of part-time attendance in a public school. Intraschool activities may eliminate the problem of belonging, but they may heighten the issue of division of loyalties.

Certainly, the pupil should be encouraged to feel that he belongs to both schools and that he is not a guest at one of them. There is not necessarily a relationship between shared time and a feeling of divided loyalties, but administrators and teachers should be on guard to prevent or minimize problems of this nature.

What Are Some School-Community Relations Problems?

Public and parochial schools have become integral features of the American tradition. In the interest of the common good, they *cannot* be enemies. They must, and often do, cooperate well with each other. As stated before, this cooperation is the key to any successful shared-time endeavor, but the important question of community reactions must be considered.

Even with the best of intentions, shared-time proposals can

become issues which divide communities into warring factions. How will a community react if shared-time practices result in major schedule changes and/or an extended school day for some public school students? How will community members react to changes in the transportation schedule? If the conduct of a parochial school pupil requires censure in a public school, or if the grades of a pupil involved in a shared-time program vary from his past record, the opportunities become evident for backyard experts to assess the disciplinary and academic strengths and weaknesses of public and parochial schools.

Although these types of concern are not in themselves important enough to prevent the implementation of a program of shared time, these molehills tend to grow into mountains of negativism. Great care must be exercised to present the issues as clearly and as objectively as possible in order to gain support of the many groups which comprise a community.

The community must be made ready to accept certain departures from conventional school practices. A variety of media should be used in order to reach the patrons and parents of the public and parochial schools. The local nature of the administration of shared-time programs requires as thorough an understanding as possible by all community residents. In too many communities the school informs its patrons of what it deems important and provides no inlet for response. This selective, one-way communications pattern has long been criticized by students of school administration but the practice continues. The issues at stake now are too important and too volatile for school officials, whether public or parochial, to decide in a vacuum. The citizens must be permitted and encouraged to inform the school officials of their laymen's views, and means must be made available for the airing of these views. Open meetings with open agendas, variations on the "suggestion box" and "letters-to-the-editor" ideas, telephone contacts, newspaper coverage, television and radio forums and panels representing informed but diverse views are but a few means of opening the two-way channel of communications between the schools and their patrons.

Issues related to the shared-time concept not only may force the schools to improve their community relations program, but also may highlight the necessary cooperation between public and parochial school officials involved in shared-time practices. If effective, this cooperation can unite communities so that a strong concerted effort can be made toward the overall improvement of education.

Who Is Legally Responsible for the Pupils?

It is easy to say that the school where the pupil is in attendance is legally responsible for his safety and welfare. If the pupil attends a public school in the morning, that school is responsible for him until the afternoon, when the parochial school assumes the responsibility. However, the question arises about the overlapping time and the "time void." If the pupil attends a public school until noon, does the legal responsibility for that school end at noon *exactly?* If not, when does it end, and when does the responsibility of the parochial school begin? Even if the two schools are willing to share the responsibility for the pupil, an injury can create complicated legal problems.

The question of legal responsibility for pupil transportation is unanswered. If pupil and parochial school children are combined into one group at the public school for the purpose of a trip to an art museum where the works of French artists are on display, is this a field trip for the French class (public school jurisdiction) or for the art class (parochial jurisdiction)? In case of an accident which results in legal action, which school is responsible if damages are awarded?

The entire matter of pupil accountability can be thrown into confusion in a shared-time program. Truancies, legitimate absences, and tardinesses must be the proper concerns of both the participating public and parochial schools. Although the specifics of the legal responsibility for pupil accountability may not be clearly defined, the necessity to define the areas for which both schools assume responsibility is clear.

Further insight into the solutions of these problems would have to be the result of court adjudication, but in the absence of such guides administrators should plan with caution and prudence.

What Are Some of the Transportation Problems?

The administrative headaches involved in working out details of the transportation schedule in relation to the curriculum schedule are already well known. Participation in a shared-time program can add to these headaches in terms not only of schedule concerns but also of cost factors. Questions which must be considered include the following: Which school is responsible for the purchase of buses? Are the drivers, who serve both schools, responsible to one or both schools? Who pays the drivers? Which school sets the bus schedules? Will the transportation schedules have an adverse effect upon the extracurricular activities of either the public or the parochial students?

Unless the schools involved are located close together, an ideal but rare arrangement, the cost of and the responsibility for transportation, as well as the time spent by students in traveling from one school to another, may lead to a rejection of the whole idea.

What Are Some of the Financial Factors?

Attendance for part of the day at both public and private schools can create financial problems which neither school can afford. The utilization, or lack of utilization, of facilities can become a greater financial expense than anticipated. Expanded enrollments in secular subjects for that part of the day when parochial school students attend the public school can be very costly in terms of the capital outlay for expanded facilities as well as for hidden expenses at the times when these expanded facilities are not in use.

Shared-time programs effect great financial savings in that they eliminate the need to duplicate facilities, but enormous expenditures are often necessary for the implementation of these programs, which could involve more than 5,500,000 parochial school students throughout the nation. Financial concerns involve not only facilities but teacher time, fuel, lighting, and those other expenses which were highlighted in the *McCollum* and *Zorach* cases.[1] These classic decisions may point to certain financial factors which have been interpreted officially as important.

On the positive side, the involvement of parochial school children in public school classes may result in increased support by many Catholics of public school financial issues. The complaint of "double financial effort" by Catholic parents whose children attend parochial schools may become less forceful if public school facilities are used for part of the school day by parochial students.

Conclusions and Recommendations

The foregoing questions and many more like them must be answered satisfactorily if shared-time programs are to work effectively.

Yet, in a broader sense some of the questions relate to administrative concerns even if there is a continuation of the pattern of separate public and parochial schools. Therefore, the recommendations which follow are presented for the serious consideration of public and parochial school administrators regardless of their views toward shared-time programs. The general issues are national, but the feasibility of these recommendations must be tested in terms of local effort and practices.

1. It is necessary to reexamine the whole concept of public and parochial education in terms of financial support, purposes, directions, and values.
2. Public and parochial schools should conduct an on-going program of school-community relations in order to gain the acceptance, understanding, and support of citizens for the implementation of departures from conventional school programs.
3. Each parochial school should set its own realistic limits on the number of students whom it can teach effectively, and all others should attend public schools.
4. Before communities embark upon shared-time programs, they should investigate and solve their own unique administrative problems so that the net result is not the addition of more problems than the program solves.
5. The school day and/or the school week should be expanded so that maximum use of public and parochial schools can result without expending additional funds for capital outlay.
6. Additional financial support for public and/or parochial schools should be made available through expanded state and federal aid, expanded tax base, increased state and local financial effort, and increased tuition.
7. The solutions of community problems *in general* require the close cooperation of public and parochial school leaders.

Chapter Twelve

•

WAYS THROUGH AN IMPASSE

J. RENWICK JACKSON

A dialogue is a valuable means of discovering a consensus. Listening to Protestant, Catholic and Jewish religious leaders and educators wrestle with the problems of federal aid to education and how to teach religion in the public schools, one sees the dynamic possibilities and compromises of the democratic process laid bare. Ralph Waldo Emerson, with the vision of a sage, saw that "the best part of every mind is not that which he knows, but that which hovers in gleams, suggestions, tantalizing, unpossessed before him. . . . This dancing chorus of thoughts and hopes is the quarry of his future, is his possibility." Emerson's promise was fulfilled in the imaginative sparks ignited by the free and reasoned discussion at a meeting

Dr. J. Renwick Jackson has a doctorate from the University of Edinburgh. He represented *Newsweek* at the World Council of Churches meeting in New Delhi; he has served as lecturer and consultant at both the Nippon Academy in Tokyo and the United Church of Christ in Manila. He has given the Berry Lecture at the University of Hawaii and traveled extensively in the other states. He was an Associate Director for National Program Development, the National Conference of Christians and Jews, and is now Dean of Students, Queensboro Community College, Bayside, New York.

in 1964 at Indiana University. Quarries of new understandings and possibilities have been, and are being, mined by those who are involved in the great dialogues of our time. A concrete example of results of compromise is the Elementary and Secondary School Act of 1965, discussed in Chapter Four, which opened the door for limited federal aid for youth in nonpublic schools.

Contributions of the Dialogue

There are signs that we are moving from polemics to discussion, from a propounding of particular viewpoints to an attempt to find an acceptable consensus. We are seeing more clearly that the democratic process does not end with interest groups articulating their particular concerns and protecting their rights; rather, it begins here. We must broaden our perspective to respect the rights and viewpoints of others, even when these rights conflict with our own; responsible men care about the diverse interests of the whole society and strive to harmonize those interests and conflicts into a public philosophy.

Developments in the field of federal aid to education indicate that headway is being made. In spite of continuing vindictiveness and grudging acquiescence, the force of circumstance and the patient work of enlightened men are creating a new climate of cooperation. Meeting in Columbus, Ohio, in February, 1964, with Jews and Roman Catholics participating, the Church-State Consultation of the National Council of Churches rejected the concept of an "absolute" separation of church and state; and while firmly opposing public support of sectarian religion, they endorsed the use of public funds for health and welfare programs that would meet particular needs in private and parochial schools.

A number of Roman Catholics, most notably recently Mrs. Mary Perkins Ryan, are questioning if the parochial school system has fulfilled its original purpose and are wondering if it is now time for Roman Catholics to commit themselves to public education to allow the parish and the family to concentrate on the mission of the church in society. Mrs. Ryan's book, *Are Parochial Schools the Answer?*,[1] and the responses to it reveal only the most public aspects of the dialogue that is going on within the Roman Catholic Church.

The discussion is accented by cutbacks in parochial education. For example, Father Neil McCluskey reports that:

> Because the Archdiocese of Cincinnati faced a financial crisis, it would probably be necessary to drop the first four grades from Cincinnati Catholic Schools. . . . A few weeks earlier the Rochester Diocese had announced that after September there would be a ban on new Catholic schools and on expansion of existing schools for the immediate future. A year earlier, the Cardinal-Archbishop of St. Louis had laid down a similar policy for his archdiocese. The bishops of Saginaw, Spokane, Kansas City, Fargo, Richmond and Green Bay have all been forced to adjust to the shortage of teachers and classrooms by curtailing one or more of the grades in their schools.[2]

Of course, these comments and decisions need to be seen within the context of a strong Roman Catholic commitment to parochial schools.[3]

Public policy is also becoming more flexible toward federal aid to education. The state of Rhode Island is lending textbooks without charge to students in private schools. Matching grants of public funds to Roman Catholic and Protestant church-related colleges have been given by the state of Maryland. The Higher Education Facilities Act of 1963 provides 1.2 billion dollars, a portion to be used by nonpublic colleges and universities to build libraries or classrooms designed specifically for the teaching of natural or physical sciences, mathematics, foreign languages, or engineering. The extension of the National Defense Education Act gives considerable support already, and the possibilities of aid in President Johnson's war on poverty have enlarged the commitment of the federal government to nonpublic education.

Educational experiments are equally significant. In numerous communities high school voluntary summer programs for nonpublic school students, educational TV, and most promising of all, shared time, offer cooperative possibilities between public and nonpublic schools. In several cities boards of education are also effectively using the dialogue in the difficult areas of school integration and bus transportation.

There is a correlation between community dialogue and diminished tensions and violence. Although we are in the early stages of exploration, the examples that we have cited may prove to be inadequate or even wrong solutions. At this point the answers to the problems posed by federal aid to education are unknown. But the significant fact is that these first steps represent cooperative attempts. They demonstrate the value of the dialogue as a process by which we can enlarge our sympathies with others' problems and concerns. These discussions, as Dr. Eberhard Müller, the Director of the Bad Boll Academy near Stuttgart, has emphasized, "have a warming and life-giving force if their purpose is not the intellectual liquidation of opponents but communication between those jointly seeking answers. Such discussions can lay the groundwork for free cooperation between many individuals. In a cooperative society the cultivation of such discussion is increasingly demonstrating its validity as the decisive instrument for the nurture of freedom and of man himself."[4]

The Dilemma

A second reflection is more complex. Concurring with the judgment of the Supreme Court that devotional prayers and Bible readings in the public schools are unconstitutional, Justice Brennan wrote that

> The holding of the Court today plainly does not foreclose teaching about the Holy Scriptures or about the differences between religious sects in classes in literature or history. Indeed, whether or not the Bible is involved, it would be impossible to teach meaningfully many subjects in the social sciences or the humanities without some mention of religion. To what extent, and at what points in the curriculum religious materials should be cited, are matters which the courts ought to entrust very largely to the experienced officials who superintend our nation's public schools. They are expert in such matters and we are not.[5]

The National Council of Churches issued a policy statement in which they declared that "the public schools have an obligation to help individuals develop an intelligent understanding and appreciation of the role of religion in the life of the peoples of this nation."[6] But their statement also poses the dilemma: "attempts to establish a 'common core' of religious beliefs to be taught in public schools have usually proven unrealistic and unwise. Major faith groups have not agreed on a formulation of religious beliefs common to all. Even if they had done so, such a body of religious doctrine would tend to become a substitute for the more demanding commitments of historic faiths."[7]

Herein is the dilemma: public educators are told by religious leaders that they have an obligation to help individuals develop an intelligent understanding of the role of religion but are also told that there is no curriculum, or "common core," available by which they can do it. I sympathize with the school superintendent who said, "Our job is difficult enough without taking on the problems of religion; let's get the church off the back of public education."

The Complexity of Religion

The problem is as complex as religion itself. There is the historical study of religious traditions which attempts to understand the role of religion in culture. This study always reveals the ambiguity of religion, the ways in which it has both blessed and cursed the life of man.

Then there is the institutional expression of religion which calls for a commitment to a particular community, dogma, ritual, ethic.

Third, there is religion as a way of life, an attitude or perspective, an awareness of meaning, which may or may not be related to an institutional commitment. This expression has received much contemporary affirmation. Dietrich Bonhoeffer, victim of Nazi execution, called for a new community of "religionless Christianity," and the late Paul Tillich has often stated that the first word to be spoken by authentic faith is a word against religion. Many people are growing aware of the distinction between communion with God and its identification with any particular forms.

The Religious Responsibility of Public Education

This diversity of religious understanding accents the public educator's frustration when he considers teaching about religion in the public schools. It is necessary therefore to clarify the functions of public education and religious institutions.

No person is educated who remains uninformed about the history of religion and its significance in human experience. The Educational Policies Commission affirmed this position in their statement that "knowledge about religion is essential for a full understanding of our culture, literature, art, history, and current affairs."[8] Alfred North Whitehead, in his essay, *The Aims of Education*, goes further in stating that "the essence of education is that it be religious." By this he meant that

> a religious education is an education which inculcates duty and reverence. Duty arises from our potential control over the course of events. Where attainable knowledge could have changed the issue, ignorance has the guilt of vice. And the foundation of reverence is this perception, that the present holds within itself the complete sum of existence, backwards and forwards, that whole amplitude of time, which is eternity.[9]

Whether or not we understand or like his language, his viewpoint is worthy of consideration. It expresses the classical view that education is not merely the accumulation of facts but the hammering out of an informed understanding of the meaning of human existence and a living out of that meaning. This is clearly the task of public education, and educators should reject every attempt to limit their work to technical training. The teaching vocation can be supplied with valuable resources through the historical study of religion, the meanings which it has had for mankind, and the ways in which these meanings have permeated every aspect of culture.

Relations of Public and Religious Education

As the statement of the National Council of Churches pointed out, the development of such a curriculum and the training of teachers to teach it might "tend to become a substitute for the more demanding commitments of historic faiths," and protests from some representatives of religious institutions will arise. In response, public educators can assure these churchmen that their concern is understood and honored. Second, the nonsectarian teaching of the history of religion is human history and is properly the task and responsibility of public education. Third, a large portion of American citizens, at least one third, a minimal estimate, have no relationship with any religious community, while many more who may have such affiliation receive no serious religious education. If these persons are to receive any understanding of religion, it will be provided only by the public school. Fourth, while this nonsectarian teaching about religion will not aim to influence attitudes toward religion, we are aware that objective knowledge about religion may contribute to a stronger religious commitment for some persons and will prepare all students for a more intelligent and responsible participation in a pluralistic society. Fifth, churchmen can be assured that the task of religious education, that is, educating for commitment to God and to a particular tradition, is properly the function of religious communities.

The religious community, however, can exercise no monopoly of teaching about religion; neither can there be ecclesiastical or clerical encroachment on public institutions; nor can public institutions be expected to assist in the task of religious education. These desires represent a failure to understand the peculiar educational task of the religious communities; further, they reveal fears that the teaching about religion will provide substitutes for historic faiths, or that if public institutions do not assist the religious communities in their work, the churches and synagogues will lose ground in an increasingly secular society.

Anxiety often clouds perspective. In this situation it is important for religious people to see clearly the supplementary and constructive functions that public education can fulfill by teaching about religion in a pluralistic society and to remember the faithfulness of God and the power of the historic faiths, which have weathered all kinds of transitions.

A vital religious community should expect and will require

no more than a favorable environment of religious liberty. Our society provides such a climate plus extra benefits such as tax exemptions. If primitive Christianity could thrive in the face of social persecution and martyrdom, if the blood of the martyrs could be the seed of the church, if religious communities in East Germany and the Soviet Union can flourish in the face of hostility and discrimination, surely the religious communities in the United States require no public assistance to achieve their purposes. The American experience demonstrates that a favorable neutrality in church-state relations offers special advantages in which religion can flourish. The point is well taken that the church has more to fear from Constantine than it does from Nero, which is to say that the corruptions of establishment are more perilous than persecution.

The opposite tack is for religious leaders to charge the public schools with being godless and secular and to use this critique to support the need for religious schools. But it is important to remember that this criticism can cut both ways, for it acknowledges that religious communities have been ineffective in their relations to public education and that they have tended to abdicate responsibility within the public schools. This position fails to appreciate that secularization has often been a means of liberating mankind from the burdens of religious ignorance, superstition, and oppression, and that the attitudes of religious isolationism or imperialism perpetrate the worst abuses of both religious and secular life.

Religious communities and men of faith will never be satisfied with a rigid separation between public and religious education. While it is necessary to distinguish a division of special function, God and truth and life cannot be fragmented; religious knowledge can never finally be partitioned from religious commitment. Religious communities and men of faith need to find ways to express their convictions in a pluralistic society.

The Ministry of the Laity

How can this expression be made? Perhaps the answer is to be found in our renewed awareness of the churches and synagogues as the people of God who are to be a community of reconciliation and service in society. In a pluralistic society the ministry of the laity* may be the strategic means of fulfilling this vocation and the new dimension which will enable us to find creative associations between church and state. At least it will invigorate the polarized situation becaues it shifts our attention from institutions, buildings, clergy, to people, many of whom are already involved in influential positions in public institutions. Emphasizing this viewpoint, Professor Heinz-Dietrich Wendland in his penetrating book *Die Kirche in der Modernen Gesellschaft* wrote:

> In this new era of its encounter with the world, the church should neither try to integrate the whole world in itself nor attempt to become the predominant institution and set the pattern. In the world which has come of age the church will renounce any claim to clerical domination and any attempt to "churchify" the world, not because it is forced to do so, but because it has realized the true nature of its ministry to the world. The new attitude of the church to the world will, then, have to be one of service.[10]

Since the Second World War there has been a great deal of discussion about the ministry of the laity; increasingly religious communities have been affirming that the laity are the means whereby the churches and synagogues can participate in the decision-making of a pluralist society. This viewpoint stresses the dual rhythm of the religious community's life: the people of God gather to worship and prepare themselves for their vo-

---

* Laity comes from the Greek word *laos*, which means people. It will be used to refer to the people of God.

cations in society; in their places of involvement they serve the public interest.

If the laity are to carry out this vocation they will need, as Klaus von Bismarck, the director of the West German Broadcasting Company, has noted, "opportunities within the life and structure of the churches where [they] can critically reconsider the accepted criteria, norms and customs in church and world."[11] Because of their preoccupation with institutional interests, the religious communities have failed to provide sufficient opportunities for these considerations. As a result the laity are unprepared for and in many cases unaware of this vocation.

The failure reveals a slowness to develop new strategies for new situations, a condition which religious institutions share with other organizations. A parallel may be found in the sluggish adaptation that the military establishment has made from traditional techniques of warfare to guerrilla combat. Underlining this need for adaptation, Miss Molly Batten, principal of William Temple College in Rugby, England, declares that "the aim of the churches must be to minimize the cost of the bases in order to maintain the maximum number of men in operations. . . ."[12]

Training for the Laity

More important than past failures, the religious communities are beginning to provide training for the laity. The pioneering leadership emerged in Germany at the end of World War II. In the small university town of Tubingen two men spent some of the last long nights of the war discussing what could be done for the spiritual reconstruction of Germany. One was theologian Helmut Thielicke, driven out of his professorship by the Nazis, and the other was university pastor Eberhard Müller, who had just been released from a prisoner of war camp in

Russia. These men had watched the failure of political and social organizations during Hitler's seizure of power and the subsequent disintegration of their country. They knew that the church had almost no influence on the complicated mechanisms of modern mass society, that its influence had shrunk to the narrow circle of home and neighborhood and that it no longer exercised its responsibility in the decisive areas of culture.

Searching for a way to involve themselves in these problems, the two theologians conceived a plan for creating a center where the different groups of the German people could discuss their problems. The first conference, concerned with the realization of justice in political life, took place in September, 1945. Conferences for workers, farmers, church leaders, soldiers, journalists, teachers, and other vocations followed. The first conference for workers received poor response because the invitations were sent through local parishes; after this, favorable results were achieved by sending the invitations through secular institutions.

The gatherings start with discussions of the practical problems of people in modern society. In an open atmosphere optimists, cynics, atheists and persons of faith participate in discussions, listen to each other, and forthrightly speak their convictions. Dialogue is basic; the hope is that understanding and mutual respect will be increased and that progress will be made toward a public consensus.

While these academies have exercised a widespread influence in Germany, their impact has been world-wide. There are more than fifty academies in Europe including centers in Norway and Sicily; they have formed a European association and publish a newsletter. The Columbus Group is a similar organization in the U.S.A.; new academies are emerging all over the world in places such as Northern Rhodesia, India and Japan. To many of us the academy movement is the most exciting and relevant expression in the renewal of the church, for in the words of Eberhard Müller, the academies try "to put the Christian message without the forms that customarily surround it in the church simply and directly into the problematic of everyday life. Where this is done successfully, even this centuries-old message will not seem strange or forced. This message will then appear as the most necessary part of the discussion concerning modern life, the part that points the way to ultimate answers."

Similar ventures have been undertaken by the Roman Catholics. The University of San Francisco has established a center to train laymen in the nature and mission of the church; these laymen are then assigned to parishes where they help other laymen to be responsible in their occupations and public involvements. The Jesuits have organized the founding of the John LaFarge Institute in midtown New York, where Catholic leaders, with the cooperation and fellowship of all men of good will, will seek to alleviate group tensions and contribute to the solution of community problems. Institutes of study and social action have been founded by Roman Catholic orders all around the world in places such as Manila and La Paz, Bolivia. The Institute in La Paz was founded by a group of Roman Catholic lay leaders and its activities will be divided into four sections: socio-economic research, leadership training, social action, and religious problems.

The People of God in Public Affairs

What does it mean to be the people of God in public affairs? There are few blueprints with ready-made formulations; the centers are places of dialogue where people wrestle with the issues of their lives and vocations and discover for themselves what this means. But there is some general consensus: that we are the people of God in the whole of life; that God is interested not only in religious institutions but in the great issues of our history; that there is a mystery in human destiny and that every person has worth and dignity; that the contemporary battles of truth and justice are our battles; that our primary commitment is to the common welfare even when it means risking our own interests; that encompassing our existence is the presence and love of the Eternal Spirit, who faithfully gives us resources of compassion and courage for these tasks and staying power when we are battered and our objectives are defeated.

V. K. Matthew, an Indian lawyer, describing the ministry of the laity in politics, put it this way:

> The church must teach its laity the necessity for legitimate forms of compromise in political life. One type of legitimate compromise is to effect adjustment of convictions in order to arrive at purposeful general consensus. Another form of compromise may be to live with corruption in the same party. The accent in all these cases should not be on keeping oneself pure and undefiled but on how one can most effectively serve the real welfare of the community.[13]

This accents the fact that for men of faith there will be necessary differences in language and style of life in the religious communities and in public involvements. In the former it will be worship; in the latter it will be service. Of course life cannot be divided; service may be worship but in a secular society this will be evident in attitude rather than ritual.

A concrete example of this responsible participation in public institutions was lived out by a man of faith in local political action in a town of twenty-five thousand people. Making known his concern about the political process, he managed to get a party endorsement as a candidate for the City Council and through hard and clever campaigning was elected by a

plurality of thirty-eight votes. A number of citizens continued
to work with him in the reform of local government. Using
the newspapers and radio-TV, they informed their fellow citizens about what was happening in their community. The Planning Board and Board of Adjustment were pressured into vot-
ing on public issues in open meetings. As people became informed, it was increasingly difficult for things to slip through,
especially those actions that were contrary to the welfare of
the city.

This group has again and again fought irresponsible, under-
the-table deals. For example, an attempt was made to give the
contract for the hospitalization of city employees to an agent
who was twelve thousand dollars above the lowest bid. Several
unethical factors came to light; the agent with the high bid had
been selected before the Council met; discrepancies in the bids
suggested that they had been tampered with; special benefits
were included for retired councilmen.

An attempt was made to build a large apartment house in an
area of residential homes. One hundred and fifty residents of
the area protested against the plan; the Council passed it any-
way. The Citizens instituted court action; the Court was unable
to rule on the issue because the minutes of the Board of Adjustment disappeared. The issue went back to the Council, which
voted it again; the citizens took it to court again; this time the
Court upheld the citizens. A councilman who had supported
the building of the apartment house was defeated in his attempt
for reelection to the Council. Finally, houses were built in that
area. This kind of honest, responsible political presence has
made a valuable contribution to the welfare and health of this
community.

Similar kinds of responsible participation need to be given by
educators, public officials, and citizens in educational institutions.
If citizens, including men of faith, would approach the prob-

lems of education with concern for the welfare of the whole community, and if men of faith would express their particular concern in responsible actions rather than sectarian interests, the deeper issues of religion and education could be clarified.

These issues are more profound than public funds for private education or devotional exercises in public schools; they have to do with philosophies of education and truth, with the nature of humanity, with the meaning and values of life, and with ways in which these realities may be fulfilled.

Religious communities on the whole have been derelict in engaging in these great dialogues. Sectarian education has tended to withdraw from the public battlefields and carry on the educative process in cloisters or has tried to use public institutions or monies for self-centered interests. The vocation of the laity as responsible participants in public institutions opens new possibilities which may move us forward through the impasse. At least the great dialogues will be ignited.

If the religious communities are to provide occasions for dialogue that Klaus von Bismarck calls for, and if they are to equip and support their members for the responsibilities that Mr. Matthew describes, religious institutions will have to provide new patterns of education for the laity; the churches and synagogues will have to mobilize their resources and refuse to be diverted to tangential activities. Failure to meet the challenges of this new situation will probably relegate the religious communities to the peripheral edges of society and deprive our nation of those unique contributions which they have to share.

Ways Through the Impasse

Perhaps we have come full circle. Public educators should undertake their responsibility to teach about religion in the public schools; religious educators should participate in the reform of religious institutions in order that the laity may be equipped to be the people of God in public affairs. Educators who are members of religious communities have both challenges—to catalyze reforms in religious institutions and to be the people of God in public education so that, while respecting the academic disciplines and freedoms of our public schools, they may enrich the great dialogues about the meaning of human existence and assist public education to fulfill its mandate and its dream.

In so doing the favorable neutrality between church and state will be maintained; public education will include teaching about religion; the particular commitments of the religious communities, through the laity, will contribute to the great public dialogues; the prophetic judgments of pluralistic diversity will save us from the tyrannies of fanaticism, sectarianism, secularism, and national idolatry. The religious communities, faithful to their traditions and open to their futures, and public education, center of opportunity and responsibility, will provide the raw materials of a public philosophy.

The lag between these hopes and present reality shocks us out of any tendencies toward utopianism and encourages a humble recognition of human limitations. A possible image of the various interest groups in our society could be one of icebergs, solid and frozen, with a danger of damaging collisions. But icebergs can, to some extent, melt and contribute to the oceans that carry great vessels to their destinations. At least, by way of prevention, modern radar equipment can minimize the dangers of collision.

The currents of change are harbingers of a new era. Could it be that through these strategies the dialogues between past, present, and future, between particular traditions and new challenges, can forge that free and good society whose laws and values will facilitate the fulfillment of human life?

Chapter Thirteen

•

ACCOMMODATIONS TO RELIGIOUS PLURALISM

After Bible reading and prayer, no other exercise or occasion in the public schools provides so much difficulty for those who recognize that even a multidenominational religion may not be "established" than does Christmas.

Christmas has come to be a joyous and festive season in America. At the same time in the commercial world it is now the big selling season. Carols are sung in banks and railroad stations. Public address systems ring out with Christmas music. Long before December first, shopping centers and main streets are decorated, and bells jingle on every downtown corner. Radio and television programs going out over the nonsectarian ether build up to the big day. Village greens, commons, and squares are aglow with Christmas trees and lights. Half the nation follows breathlessly the erection and lighting

This chapter is reprinted from *Religion in the Public Schools,* a publication of the American Association of School Administrators. It is part of a report by the Commission on Religion in the Public Schools, whose chairman was Sidney P. Marland, Jr., Superintendent of Schools in Pittsburgh, Pennsylvania. We wish to thank the Association for permission to use part of its report.

of the huge tree at Rockefeller Plaza, or the municipal tree downtown. The "national" tree in Washington blazes at the touch of the President's finger on the button. Christmas is everywhere.

Yet two sets of voices are increasingly being raised in protest. Some Christian religious leaders passionately protest the growing commercialization and secularization of the Advent. Christmas, they remind us, is a religous event, a true holy day which celebrates the birth of Him whose name it bears and whom they serve. They fear that this central fact gets blurred and diffused in the secular customs with which the day has become encrusted.

Another group speaks for the millions of Americans of different religions or philosophies. They protest the all-pervasive Christmas. They do not begrudge their Christian brothers' celebrations, but do protest the air of official support inherent in the use of governmental funds and agencies in the celebrations. They want to protect their young people from growing to feel that they are second-class citizens in a country which, professing no establishment of religion, seems in fact annually to endorse and support one. Particularly are they sensitive to the atmosphere and activities in the public schools which are their children's principal contact with government, and in which they learn by precept and practice the rights and responsibilities of citizenship.

A third group, in many American communities the largest one, likes things as they are. They are especially sensitive to any possibility of change in those public schools in which Christmas customs have grown almost into tradition. They come from no single denomination. Their own beliefs are diverse. Yet they have in common a concern lest something be lost in the change.

It is hard to arrive at a resolution of the problems at any

time, and usually almost impossible in the Christmas season itself. But calm reflection away from the almost-frenzy of the Christmas season may lead to a better understanding of the dangers as seen by both the protesting groups and the protectors of local tradition. At other seasons it is easier to think as citizens, to reexamine our Constitutional compact, to understand again why it is that in America we cannot have an establishment of religion—even of a sort of vaguely nondenominational Christianity.

There have not been many cases in our courts which bear specifically on Christmas celebrations in the public schools, although the basic law does seem clear. Under the Constitution, the public schools may not sponsor a religious service or service of worship, whether it be for a single or multidenominational group. Neither may public schools support or promote the Christian religions, Christian churches, nor distinctively Christian doctrines either exclusively or along with other religions, churches, and their distinctive doctrines.

In nearly all school districts, the following four generalizations seem warranted, and must be considered in making policy.

1. By long custom and nearly universal practice, the Christmas season has a special significance both in community custom and folk culture. The schools may not without violating the principles of learning ignore this element in the children's environment. Further, in drama, music, and art there is a very large body of works related to the Christmas theme and season that have entered into the Western world's culture.

2. Many Christian religious leaders deplore strongly the modern tendency "to take the Christ out of Christmas" and hence oppose secularized and nonreligious observances of

one of Christianity's holiest days, whether in the public schools or elsewhere.

3. The celebration of the birth of Christ is almost unique in the degree to which it is shared by enrolled members of every Christian denomination and by many without formal church affiliations. It enlists a larger majority of our citizens and touches individuals and families in that majority more centrally than does any other holy day.

4. Public school teachers and administrators are by their profession sensitive to the needs and interests of children in society, and by their office responsible for understanding and supporting the laws of the land. In Christmas they are faced with an occasion that is based on doctrinal religion, which many of them hold deeply. It is strongly charged emotionally with tenderness towards children, which they share especially. It is not covered specifically and in detail by clear-cut guides. And it is encrusted with tradition and reinforced by widespread governmental example (White House Christmas Tree, for one) to support that tradition.

In the light of these generalizations, the issues can be narrowed somewhat. A public school, whatever the feelings of its constituents, may not observe Christmas as though it were a church or combination of churches. On the other hand an educational institution for children may not, consistent with proven educational principles of readiness and interest, ignore Christmas. Finally, the good public school will be highly sensitive to its obligation to support and protect the religious development of every child in its charge, in whatever religious tradition he and his family embrace. In this last may be found the key to sound policy.

The non-Christian is not a guest in a Christian school—he is a fellow citizen in a public school which includes a good many Christian members. His customs and beliefs are not shared by as many of his fellows as share the Christian traditions, usually, but he finds the public school a place and school teachers and administrators the kind of people who welcome him for himself, whatever his beliefs or his family's faith. He grows in love and respect for a school and a governmental system which cherish diversity, including religious diversity, while it supports each member's faith and belief without preferment. The message of peace on earth and good will among men is given real meaning.

At school the child will sing more songs from the Christian heritage—not as a worshiper, of course—because there *are* more and he joins the others in wanting to share them. But some of the music will be in his own religious tradition on appropriate occasions for the same reasons. He may dance around a gaily decorated tree, or learn about wassailing, or about gift-giving—these are pre-Christian or pagan in origin and common to many societies. He may be enthralled with Dickens' *Christmas Carol* or other stories about Christmas. But he will not find himself an outsider at a Christmas service. Neither will he fail to distinguish between these cultural trimmings and the essential holiness to Christians of the celebrations that take place in their own homes and churches, where they will find the holy day and worship the Holy Child. He will understand and respect the home and church traditions of others because he has his own events of spiritual-ethical-religious significance in his way of life, which he celebrates at home or in his place of religious gathering. In turn he will enjoy the understanding and respect of others.

The Commission can make no prescription. It can only suggest the limitations and point out the spirit within which solutions must be found. It suggests that what is best for a given community, even for an individual school, will not come as a compromise among religious views, nor as a vector from varying pressures. Rather will it come from the careful planning, school by school, of programs that fall within the obvious limits and that reflect the considered concern for the maximum growth of children in a religiously diverse school and society.

In a public school which has regularly found occasions for children to tell about their own and hear about others' religious celebrations, rites, and beliefs, few problems arise. The teacher sets the atmosphere. He or she need only be warmly interested and supportive for children to see that their differing customs and beliefs are neither strange nor the cause for estrangement but are rather wonderful and essential elements of a pluralistic society. The trap for the teacher who has not deliberately thought through his own role lies in his unconscious identification with one of the religions or groupings of religions. How easy it is for a committed Christian to speak of "we" and "our" ways, unconsciously thereby leading children to identify the "we" with the school and government or world, and perhaps themselves with the outcast or minority "they"! It becomes hard for them then to see that the schools and the government do not belong to Congregationalists or Catholics or Baptists or Adventists or Jews or Ethical Culturists or Humanists or Atheists—but to the people as citizens with their citizenship in common, whatever their religious diversities.

There is a vast difference in spirit and effect between a school's "own" Christmas pageant or Christmas displays on the one hand, and an exposition by some children to other children of their family, cultural, and church customs and rites, when it is one of a series of expositions at appropriate times of differing customs and rites designed to build a common appreciation of the many religious contributions to our heritage, on the other hand. The former is establishment of religion, the assertion of "a" school religion. The latter is a recognition of the deep importance to each child of his own religion and to all people of the varying religious commitments of their fellow citizens.

Even if or perhaps especially when a particular school might appear to be made up exclusively of children of one religious affiliation, their citizenship development requires that they learn that other citizens of their community, state, and nation have other affiliations while sharing equally as citizens.

The Commission recommends the policy that encourages reasonable recognition of Christmas in the schools in the spirit of exposition of the differing rites and customs of families, cultures, and creeds—each with deep meaning for its adherents, and in sum revealing the many different religious, philosophical, and cultural practices and beliefs held by Americans.

The public schools are and of a right should be responsive to their communities, within constitutional and other relevant limits. But they also have uniquely the commitment to teach the meaning, the obligations, and the rights of citizenship, including the necessity for protection against the establishment of religion and against intrusion on the religious freedoms of any and all citizens in the United States. In such a context, Christmas in the schools becomes a manageable problem and a potential asset.

The School Calendar and Individual Religious Obligations

There is no calendar which perfectly meets all of the different needs for marking the passage of time. However, in most of the more advanced nations of the world there is now a common civil calendar which takes into account the solar and lunar cycles with considerable accuracy. This calendar, the Gregorian, was worked out under the patronage of Pope Gregory XIII and promulgated in 1582. It was adopted in England 170 years later and in the American colonies at the same time. For the first time the seasons fell in the same calendar segments and the equinox was pinned to a very narrow range of days in the fall and spring. This is the calendar used in the civil and business affairs of all "Christian" and many other nations.

Although Pope Gregory established Christmas as December 25th and many of the events of the Christian church year fall on fixed calendar dates in relation to Christmas, neither the Christian church calendar nor that of any other religious group coincides exactly with the civil calendar.

On the Christian church calendar, Easter is what is called a movable feast date. For each civil calendar year, the date of Easter is established according to a complex formula which is related to the first full moon after the vernal equinox. The formula is an elaborate one and complicated further by an occasional artificially established equinox date, and by the fact that when the date for Easter would coincide with the first day of Passover it is moved to the following Sunday. Because of these provisions, Easter is observed on a Sunday which falls on the civil calendar on dates which, according to the *Encyclopedia Americana*, range between March 22nd and April 25th.

Christian holy days whose dates are related directly to the date of Easter include Ash Wednesday, the fortieth day before Easter; Palm Sunday, the Sunday before Easter; Holy (Maundy) Thursday, the Thursday before Easter; Good Friday, the third day before Easter; Ascension Day, the fortieth day after Easter (a Thursday); and Pentecost (Whitsunday), the fiftieth day (a Sunday) after Easter.

Fixed dates in the several Christian church calendars, many related to Christmas, include the Feast of the Immaculate Conception, December 8; the first Sunday in Advent, the fourth Sunday before Christmas; All Saints Day, November 1; the

Feast of the Circumcision, January 1; the Feast of the Epiphany, January 6; and the Feast of the Assumption, August 15. For some Protestant denominations Reformation Day, October 31, is also a significant day.

Sunday has a special legal place in the civil calendar. The Supreme Court has upheld certain Blue Laws on the grounds that basically Sunday has come to be "a day of rest" in the secular world. Because of this, the holy days of the Christian church which fall on Sunday have no effect on the school calendar, except as they may affect out-of-school activities. Christmas and New Year's Day also enjoy a special status as legal holidays. Of the other holy days, with the growing exception of Good Friday and excepting that Saturday is observed as the Sabbath by certain Christian as well as by Jewish denominations, the past practice of the churches has been to schedule religious observances and obligations in such a way as to require no interruption to the normal working or school day. In some localities more recently, a few churches have scheduled children's activities on certain holy days at times that conflict with the school day.

The Jewish calendar is not directly related to the civil calendar. It received its present fixed form from Hillel II in about 360 A.D. Although most holy days fall on a date which is fixed on the Jewish calendar, there are a few which shift slightly to make a harmonious arrangement.

The most striking fact about the Jewish calendar is that there is a periodic addition of one whole month to bring the year back into relationship with the solar and lunar cycles every nineteen years. This puts the Jewish New Year (Rosh Hashanah) on a civil calendar date that, according to a table in the *Jewish Encyclopedia*, ranges between September 6 and October 5, and affects other holy days accordingly.

Webster's New International Dictionary lists ten holidays observed in Judaism, most of which include more than one day. The B'nai B'rith Memo and Date Book (a valuable desk calendar with a glossary of holidays, available through that organization) lists and describes these:

> In the Jewish tradition, the day lasts from sunset to sunset; thus the Jewish Sabbath and all other Jewish holidays begin [at sunset] on the evening preceding the day of observance. Major Jewish festivals include Rosh Hashanah, Yom Kippur, Pesach, Shevuoth, and Sukkoth. On these holidays, Jewish children may be absent from school depending on synagogue and home requirements and practices.

In the observance of Jewish holy days, as distinct from Christian holy days other than Sunday at least, it should be noticed that the observance requires the person's presence at home or in his synagogue for much longer periods; in effect one either gives the whole day to the observance or does not observe it.

Other religions use other calendars, although the Orthodox Church calendar is similar to the Gregorian calendar.

The public school calendar varies from state to state and even from district to district within the state. It is usually governed by some fundamental legislative requirement for the number of days school is to be in session, as well as by other statutes which require the schools to observe special days, some by closing. In contrast to a calendar of working days in the business and industrial world, the typical public school calendar is established not so much by specifying the holidays as it is by designing a schedule of days on which school shall be in session that will meet the state requirements for the number of school days and will be compatible with the civil and, in some cases, church calendars.

Most public school calendars, including calendars of out-of-school activities, are almost entirely shaped to the Christian holy days. Besides the legally established holidays, many public schools do not now operate on Good Friday, for example. A small but increasing number of school districts have also tried to take into account the church calendars of other groups significantly represented in the district, although adaptation to the Jewish church calendar is made difficult by the wide range of movement of the holy days and the varying versions of Judaism.

Some school districts have tried to make provisions for at least the first day of Rosh Hashanah, a two-day festival; Yom Kippur; and occasionally the first day of Sukkoth, which is an eight-day festival—all of which regularly fall in or near September. In addition they often take into account the first day of Pesach (Passover), an eight-day festival which always falls very close to the Christian Easter. Less often they will recognize the first day of Shevuoth, which usually comes in June.

Since setting the annual school calendar is ordinarily a duty delegated and detailed in part by the state legislatures, the Commission here only calls attention to the problem. It urges that in the development of a district's school calendar every effort should be made to give support to the freest possible exercise of religious obligations by the children and staff.

In some years the school calendar might easily take into account both the significant Christian holy days and the most important Jewish holy days. In 1964-65, for example, Rosh Hashanah falls on Labor Day and the day following; Yom Kippur falls on Wednesday, September 16th; Pesach starts on the day before Easter and closes on the following Saturday; and Shevuoth falls on Sunday and Monday, June 6th and 7th.

The Commission recommends that the policies under which school calendars are established be such as to guarantee to the maximum the possibility of appropriate religious observances by all children and staff members, while providing at least the legal requirement for number of full days in uninterrupted session for the school itself.

Absences for Religious Observance

Personnel policies need examination. To the extent that the school calendar for teachers and employees makes demands that conflict with their religious obligations, special provisions are necessary. In practice these provisions vary greatly.

There are some districts in which Jewish teachers, for example, are not excused and in effect are prevented from observing their High Holy Days. Only a little less restrictive are other school districts where teacher absence for such purposes is permitted but only at the loss of salary.

Another arrangement is found in some school districts which permit absence for religious observance but charge that absence against the paid leave for sickness.

The Commission recommends that where the school calendar involves a conflict for people of some or any religious faiths, provision be made in school districts for staff absence without undue penalty for necessary individual religious observance. It notes that in a few districts with this sort of provision, such absence is charged against a fixed allowance for absences for "cogent personal reasons." Since there is a delicate Constitutional question involved, prudence dictates that form of allowance to lessen the possibility of the invoking of the establishment clause.

Where the school calendar does not take into account all of the principal days of religious obligation for its students, the Commission recommends that with appropriate safeguards children be freely excused on such days and that as a matter of policy no school examinations or other highly important school activity be scheduled for those days.

The nature and degree of the problem obviously varies tremendously from district to district and even from school to school within the district. There are school districts in which all children, to the extent that they participate in their religious observances, are in the same cluster of denominations. There are schools where on a Jewish holiday many or most of the teachers are out for observance, and very few of the children are out. The reverse is also true. But whatever the circumstance in a given district at a given time, the Commission recommends that policies affecting the school calendar, personnel practices, the children's religious observances be surveyed periodically, to ensure that they neither penalize nor make difficult religious observances by any or all of the people under the school's jurisdiction.

Cooperation in After-School and Out-of-School Activities

Public school educators recognize that school is only one of many agencies and forces in the educational development of the children it serves. Sound policy requires that the schools seek actively to adapt their after-school activities and out-of-school requirements to minimize conflict in children's time and interest with such church-connected activities as late afternoon religious classes, youth programs, and other obligations and opportunities provided by the churches to children outside of the formal school day and week.

Many unnecessary conflicts are avoided when communications are kept open and flowing between those who are responsible for such church-connected programs and the public school administrators. At one extreme there is the case where an all-school concert was scheduled for the very afternoon of an interfaith rally. This seems inexcusable. Such a conflict for children's loyalty and time could take place only when there was substantially no communication between the schools and the churches.

In these days when pressures for out-of-school study in connection with the school program are mounting and when the so-called extracurricular activities are flourishing, it may be impossible to avoid conflict completely. However, some districts are finding ways to minimize the competition for children's out-of-school time.

Some of the same consideration must be given to the members of the staff so that they may fulfill their own religious obligations and their families', and may continue, as is so frequently the case, to teach or otherwise serve their own religious institution's programs for children and youth.

The line between cooperation and establishment is difficult to draw. With respect to the so-called released-time programs, there are fairly clear legal guides. Historically such programs have ebbed and flowed. At their peak they enrolled only a very small fraction of the total number of public school students. The two Supreme Court decisions in this matter, along with some carefully drawn state statutes and regulations, provide guidance for such practice as is found today. The legality of released time seems to hinge pretty largely on the showing that no public resources are used and no element of coercion is present.

The Commission discovered practices in some school districts which represent a most extreme form of cooperation with groups of churches. In one county it was reported that "the superintendents of the school systems in the entire county have been actively interested in the work of the Sunday School Council." The schools grant and record school credit for attendance at Sunday School. Teachers are required to make reports, record credits, and send periodic reports to the school offices, and from them to the superintendents' offices. School resources and school support are used to encourage youngsters to attend their several Sunday Schools (including at least one Saturday School for Jewish children).

This practice is highly unusual and is subject to challenge. Since such a challenge is outside the intended scope of this report, the Commission only urges all districts to examine objectively all their forms of cooperation against the dual obligation to promote the free exercise of religion by appropriate cooperation with other agencies in the development of children, and punctiliously to avoid any semblance of religious establishment by using public resources or even subtle coercion.

One practice which the Commission endorses, subject only to Constitutional interpretations, is the setting aside of a bulletin board in the school building on which community organizations may display notices of meetings of interest to segments of the school's population including their church youth activities, all under appropriate safeguards.

Staff Composition

One of the ways of ensuring good communication and mutual understanding in the community is to have a faculty and staff who themselves represent diverse religious faiths and affiliations. Unfortunately it is common in communities of a changing complexity to find the distribution of religious affiliations within the staff becoming quite unrepresentative of the total community population. This is a matter of great delicacy and sensitive good sense. Religious discrimination in staff recruitment is forbidden in many states and probably under the Constitution. But if a staff is made up exclusively of people of the same or closely related religious backgrounds, it is evidence of one kind of religious discrimination, however unintended. If the public schools profess to teach the positive inherent values of a pluralistic society, they are all the more bound to practice those values. One way is to reflect a religious pluralism within the school's staff.

In the building of a staff the first consideration is competence, of course. But there is an analogy with school boards. A school board which is composed by conscious selection of one woman, one Catholic, one Jew, one Presbyterian, one banker, and one farmer, for example, is hardly more desirable than one which is only representative of a prevailing power structure. So it is with school staff. The Scylla of a staff all with the same religious background is at least as potentially bad as the Charybdis of one that is handpicked and minutely balanced to conform to some predetermined pattern, even a pattern of religious diversity. The productive and fair course lies somewhere between.

Too, school administrators are accustomed to dealing with problems of balance in a school staff. They often are looking for some sort of balance between men and women, balance in the geographical backgrounds, and balance in the special interests and potential contributions that elementary teachers have to make in science, music, art, and the like. Here the Commission urges only that an effective staff is one which is at least as diverse in its religious background as are the children in the schools. It could be argued that the diversity should be greater, in order to open the eyes and extend the horizons of the children. Such considerations in practice and in law must of course take second place to the overruling criterion of competence.

High School Baccalaureates

There are a number of practices and customs with religious overtones in which tradition varies sharply among school districts and among the states, and for which little specific guidance has so far been provided in Supreme Court interpretations or other legal sources. In this category fall the widespread use of high school baccalaureate services, of dedications and cornerstone layings, and of invocations at ceremonial occasions.

The baccalaureate service was borrowed directly from collegiate tradition. Many high schools and even some lower schools have adopted the custom as part of the graduation ceremonies. Although there may be some question as to the suitability of a program "of or pertaining to a bachelor's degree" for high school graduation, the more sensitive point is the avowedly religious nature of the service itself.

In school districts where some kind of baccalaureate is included as part of the graduation process it is handled in one of five ways:

1. Where there is a single dominant religious denomination, the service is often traditionally conducted in the second auditorium by the clergyman of that denomination. In these conditions the degree of denominationalism of the content will vary according to the sensitivity of the pastor. But strictly sectarian or not, it is basically a church service in a public school, and students are in effect required to participate. It would seem rather clearly to fall under the prohibitions of the First Amendment.

2. In some high schools clergymen from more than one denomination participate in a given baccalaureate, or the selection is rotated annually among some or all of the local clergymen. Implicitly, this arrangement frankly recognizes the religious and denominational nature of the service. Where the clergymen rotate the theory is that over a period of time the school's graduates will have been exposed to a number of different religions, although in practice each graduate will have had only one such exposure. This is a religious service, subject to challenge as such.

3. In other districts baccalaureate services are held under school auspices in a local church, or in annual rotation among churches that can and will provide the facility. The chief difference from custom just cited lies in the fact that the service is conducted outside of the school building itself. For both this and the preceding custom, the Constitutional question may hinge on whether the school requires its students to attend a religious service under school auspices, either within the school itself or in a local church or churches. The degree of compulsion or sponsorship and the reasons for the service—its "purpose and effect"—are factors which would seem to be critical in testing the constitutionality of these practices.

4. A few districts have sought to meet the Constitutional issue by continuing the baccalaureate service but stripping it of all directly religious content. They substitute inspirational poetry and prose for Bible reading and prayer, and a general exhortation for the baccalaureate sermon. The issue here is not one of form or of substance. Rather it is a matter of context. Because the baccalaureate is traditionally religious, the substitute service becomes, by the fact of substitution, open to question as an "establishment" of Humanism as an official religion.

5. The fifth solution is for religious groups represented by students in the graduating class to conduct baccalaureate services in their own churches and synagogues. In communities where some of the churches are accustomed to unite for special services a number of them may join in a union service for their own graduates. In others, every church will hold its own. In any case, the school does not require attendance nor does it do more than inform its seniors about this opportunity as it might about any other church-sponsored youth activity.

The Commission recommends this fifth practice as being compatible with sound Constitutional and educational policy. The school administrator, by taking personal initiative in the matter, in one step recognizes the important role of the churches in the lives of their own young people, avoids imposing any single religious point of view on a captive audience, and yet actively suggests the importance of high school graduation as a still momentous step in the young person's development.

Dedications

Dedication ceremonies are quite a different matter. A public school building represents the results of the hard work and the culmination of the selfless dreams of a good many fine people both within and outside the school staffs. It is the creation of people through their government and their taxes. It is natural for those who are most immediately concerned to breathe a prayer of thankfulness, and for all to wish to set the building apart with due ceremony for a special use. To those in the Judaeo-Christian tradition, such lines as "Except the Lord build the house, they labour in vain that build it," come to mind. To others these particular words may be unfamiliar, yet some comparable sentiment wells up from within their own tradition.

There are some who feel that it is inappropriate to dedicate in any religious terms a building which is essentially secular. They reason that the public tax dollar came from people and property with many and no religious labels, and they propose that good manners would prevent the arrogation of all good motives and noble aspirations to any single religion or group of religions.

Some of the difficulty may be eliminated by noting just what it means to "dedicate" a school. *Webster's New International Dictionary*, second edition, gives five definitions for the verb *dedicate:*

1. To devote exclusively to the service or worship of a divine being; or to sacred uses; to set apart with solemn rites . . .
2. To set apart formally or seriously to a definite use, end, or service . . .
3. To inscribe, address, or name by way of compliment, honor, or the like . . .
4. To open to present to the public formally . . . (Colloq.)
5. (Law) To give or surrender by way of dedication (sense 2).

Definitions 2 and 4 are clearly applicable, and number 3 may be. Formalities are a cherished part of community life. Those who hold high the value of public education look on the dedication ceremonial as a way of recognizing the community's response to its civil obligation, and of honoring those whose leadership and labor have culminated in the concrete embodiment of the community's aspirations. These are the worthy reasons for a dedication ceremony.

At the same time the young people who are to use the new building will profit from a ceremonious recognition of the community support not only for the building itself but also for the educational opportunities it makes possible. Altogether, there is much to be said for a formal dedication, particularly if it is consciously planned to give emphasis both to past accomplishment and future obligation.

One solution which recognizes the religious pluralism of a community is an open and honestly meant invitation to all citizens or groups of citizens to come together at a given time, each to make a dedication according to its appropriate rites and customs.

Another way, which has sound educational value, is to encourage the students to conduct a dedication ceremony which recognizes those who made the new building possible and pledges that those who use the building will do their best to justify that faith.

The Commission recommends a dedication ceremony that both recognizes and sets apart formally to a definite service— a ceremony conducted in a spirit of accommodation and good taste, and particularly one that makes students aware of the trust and confidence the community has so concretely displayed in its contribution.

Invocations

The matter of invocations and prayer at these and other ceremonials and occasions are practices in which the most careful reading of the decisions and dicta of the Supreme Court presents a confused picture.

American people have commonly experienced the courtesy of standing quietly in the presence of one whose religious manner, phrasing, and habits of prayer may be quite alien to some. To adults in a religiously pluralistic society it does not seem to be bothersome. Problems arise when the person praying seems to be an official representative for the rest in a religious matter.

On great state occasions, illustrated by the President's Inauguration, several religious leaders have often participated. Through that variety has been mirrored the much greater diversity among the citizenry. Similarly in public school occasions the inclusion of religious leaders of several different sects may be used to represent even greater diversity.

It should be noted that the public schools are in a peculiarly sensitive position because of the proper concern of parents and churches for their children's religious development and freedom from any element of coercion in behalf of a different religion.

This is an area in which true freedoms will develop slowly. It is one in which, excepting for classroom prayers, little controversy has yet arisen. So far at least, the Supreme Court has made a distinction between ceremonial occasions and the regular incorporation of school prayer.

The Commission recommends that such considerations as good manners, good taste, and a concern for the sensitivities and an awareness of the diversity of the faiths and affiliations of those present will dictate the wise course.

Multiple Religious Observances

Finally, among the practices discovered by the Commission is one found occasionally in schools which involve their children in a succession of religious observances of the holy days of a variety of sects. For example a public school with substantial Jewish membership may add an observance of Hanukkah in a mistaken effort to "balance off" the Christmas pageant. It seems clear that if one religious observance is forbidden then two or more are no better. The Commission set out under its discussion of Christmas its best judgment on more appropriate ways to build understanding and respect in all children for the religious customs and beliefs of others.

Conclusion

The Commission has taken up in turn each of many common school policies and practices on which the basic American Constitutional ideals of freedom of religion, freedom for religion, and freedom from governmental establishment of religion seem to have some bearing. In each case, the Commission has sought to locate the sensitive points and recommend only those policies and practices which in its best judgment are consistent both with educational ideals and Constitutional limitations, along with a recognition that the last word has not yet been said nor the final wisdom yet achieved.

APPENDIX

SELECTED BIBLIOGRAPHY

NOTES

APPENDIX
RELIGION AND THE PUBLIC SCHOOLS
Policy and Practice in Indiana

JOHN C. HILL

Superintendents, school board members, teachers, clergy, and the lay public are becoming increasingly conscious of public school practices and activities that might be considered religious in nature. The 1962 and 1963 decisions of the United States Supreme Court with respect to prayer and Bible reading have resulted in serious concern as to the role of public education and its relation to religion.

In the Spring of 1964, a 22-point questionnaire was mailed by the Indiana School Boards Association to superintendents in all 264 Indiana public school corporations operated by school boards. The questionnaire was designed to determine school

This appendix is abbreviated and reproduced with permission of Dr. Lorin Burt, Executive Secretary, Indiana School Boards Association, Bloomington, Indiana. Reported in *Research Bulletin for Indiana School Boards*, Indiana School Board Association, Box E, School of Education, Bloomington, Indiana, No. 14, April, 1964. Dr. Hill is a member of the faculty of Indiana State University, Terre Haute, Indiana.

board policies and also practices being followed by Indiana public schools which might be considered to have religious implications. The survey included questions relating to the following: Bible reading, prayer, singing of religious hymns, singing of Christmas carols, use of Nativity scenes, use of the Bible in the teaching of literature, released time for religious instruction on or off school property, shared-time programs, use of school facilities by religious groups, transportation of parochial school children, distribution of Gideon Bibles, Baccalaureate services on school property, and the use of clergy by schools at assembly programs or convocations.

Findings

Of the 264 questionnaires sent to Indiana school corporations, 227, or 86 per cent, were usable returns. The tables on the following pages show the results of the questionnaire. The figures in Tables II through VI are based on the responding schools.

TABLE I. NUMBER OF SCHOOL CORPORATIONS RESPONDING
TO RELIGIOUS PRACTICE; QUESTIONNAIRE GROUPED
ACCORDING TO TOTAL ENROLLMENT

Enrollment Category	*Number of Responses*
I (under 1,000)	44
II (1,001 to 2,000)	91
III (2,001 to 3,000)	38
IV (3,001 to 4,000)	20
V (4,001 to 8,000)	16
VI (8,001 to 20,000)	12
VII (over 20,000)	6
Total	227

Religious practices and school board policies. Ten items of the questionnaire were designed to identify the policies of Indiana school boards concerning specific religious practices. The respondents were requested to check one of the following for each of the ten practices: "required by board policy," "prohibited by board policy," "permitted by board policy at the teacher's or administrator's discretion," "the board has no policy, but it is practiced in one or more of our schools by one or more teachers or administrators," and "the board has no policy, and to my knowledge, it is not practiced in any of our schools by any teacher or administrator."

TABLE II. POLICY AND PRACTICE CONCERNING USE OF THE BIBLE

Practice	Required by board policy		Pro-hibited by board policy		Permitted by board policy		Board has no policy but it is practiced		Board has no policy; it is not practiced		Total
	No.	%	No.	%	No.	%	No.	%	No.	%	
Reading Bible at opening of school day	0	0.0	4	1.7	17	7.6	62	27.6	142	63.1	225
Use of Bible in teaching literature	0	0.0	1	0.4	33	15.2	108	49.8	75	34.6	217

Bible reading as an opening exercise is not required by board policy in any of the responding school corporations; four school boards, or 1.7 per cent, prohibit the practice, and seventeen, or 7.6 per cent, permit the practice. The respondents in 62, or 27.6 per cent, of the corporations indicated that the

Bible is being read in the absence of board policy in one or more of their schools. In 142 of the school corporations, or 63.1 per cent, no board policy exists, and the Bible is not read at the opening of the school day.

Similarly, none of the school boards require the use of the Bible in the teaching of literature. One school board prohibits this practice, and 33, or 15.2 per cent, have policies permitting the practice. One hundred and eight, or 49.8 per cent of the school corporations, in the absence of school board policy, use the Bible in the teaching of literature. Seventy-five, or 34.6 per cent, of the school corporations reported that the Bible is not used in their literature classes and that they do not have a policy concerning its use.

The respondents were asked if a course in the Bible is being taught for credit in their school corporation, and if so, what text is being used. The respondents in ten school corporations said that such a course is being taught. Four of these schools are using the King James version of the Bible as the text; four are using the Revised Standard version; and two school corporations are using all the versions listed (King James, Revised Standard, Douay, and the Jewish Publication Society Text).

Only two respondents reported that a course for credit in comparative religion is being taught in their school corporations. One stated that this course is offered at the adult education level and not as a part of the regular high school curriculum; the other reported that this course is taught to students in the twelfth grade.

Reciting the Lord's Prayer is not required by school board policy in any of the responding school corporations. Three school boards, or 1.4 per cent, prohibit this practice, and seventeen, or 7.6 per cent, have established policy permitting the practice. Eighty-seven school corporations, or 39 per cent, reported no board policy, but the practice of reciting the

TABLE III. POLICY AND PRACTICE CONCERNING USE OF PRAYER

Practice	Required by board policy		Pro- hibited by board policy		Permitted by board policy		Board has no policy but it is practiced		Board has no policy; it is not practiced		Total
	No.	%	No.	%	No.	%	No.	%	No.	%	
Reciting the Lord's Prayer	0	0.0	3	1.4	17	7.6	87	39.0	116	52.0	223
Reciting a prescribed prayer	0	0.0	7	3.2	6	2.8	40	18.4	164	75.6	217
Prayer led by a pupil or teacher	0	0.0	3	1.4	20	9.1	114	52.1	82	37.4	219

Lord's Prayer is followed in these schools. One hundred and sixteen, or 52 per cent, of the respondents indicated that their school boards prohibit this practice, and that the practice is not followed in their schools.

Reciting a prescribed prayer is not required by board policy in any of the responding schools. Seven, or 3.2 per cent, prohibit the practice, and six, or 2.8 per cent, permit the use of a prescribed prayer by board policy. Forty, or 18.4 per cent, of the respondents indicated that a prescribed prayer is used in the absence of board policy. One hundred and sixty-four respondents, or 75.6 per cent, indicated that in the absence of policy, prescribed prayers are not used in any of the schools in their corporations.

Similarly, prayer led by a pupil or teacher is not required by board policy in any of the responding schools. Three, or 1.4 per cent, prohibit the practice; and twenty, or 9.1 per cent, have established policy permitting the practice. One hundred and fourteen, or 52.1 per cent, of the respondents indicated that prayer led by a pupil or teacher is used in the absence of board policy. Several of these commented that grace is said at the noon meal. Eighty-two, or 37.4 per cent, indicated that in the absence of policy, prayer led by a pupil or teacher is not used in any of the schools in their corporation.

TABLE IV. POLICY AND PRACTICE CONCERNING SINGING OF
RELIGIOUS HYMNS, SINGING OF CHRISTMAS CAROLS,
AND USE OF NATIVITY SCENES

Practice	Required by board policy		Pro- hibited by board policy		Permitted by board policy		Board has no policy but it is practiced		Board has no policy; it is not practiced		Total
	No.	%	No.	%	No.	%	No.	%	No.	%	
Hymns	0	0.0	2	0.9	26	11.6	118	52.4	79	35.1	225
Carols	0	0.0	0	0.0	44	19.4	183	80.6	0	0.0	227
Nativity scenes	0	0.0	0	0.0	38	16.7	172	75.8	17	7.5	227

The singing of religious hymns is prohibited by board policy in two of the responding school corporations. Twenty-six, or 11.6 per cent, of the school boards permit this practice; and none of the responding school corporations require the singing of religious hymns in their schools. In 118 school corporations, or 52.4 per cent, the singing of religious hymns is practiced in the absence of a state board policy. Seventy-nine, or 35.1 per cent, of the school corporations do not perform this activity. Several respondents commented that religious hymns are only sung by the school chorus or that they are sung only in the celebration of a religious holiday.

The singing of Christmas carols is either approved by board policy or practiced without board policy in all of the responding school corporations. This practice is sanctioned by board policy in 44, or 19.4 per cent, of the responding schools, and is performed in the absence of policy in all others—183, or 80.6 per cent, of the responding school corporations.

The use of Nativity scenes is approved by board policy in 38, or 16.7 per cent, of the responding school corporations. One hundred and seventy-two, or 75.8 per cent, reported this practice in the absence of stated board policy.

TABLE V. POLICY AND PRACTICE CONCERNING RELEASED TIME FOR RELIGIOUS INSTRUCTION ON AND OFF SCHOOL PROPERTY DURING THE SCHOOL DAY

Practice	Required by board policy		Pro-hibited by board policy		Permitted by board policy		Board has no policy but it is practiced		Board has no policy; it is not practiced		Total
	No.	*%*	*No.*	*%*	*No.*	*%*	*No.*	*%*	*No.*	*%*	
Released time away from school	1	.5	13	5.9	32	14.5	22	10.0	152	69.1	220
Released time on school property	1	.5	17	12.7	4	1.9	14	6.6	166	78.3	212

One school board requires that pupils be released for religious instruction away from school during the school day. In thirteen school corporations, or 5.9 per cent, this practice is prohibited by board policy; the practice is permitted by school board policy in 32 school corporations, or 14.5 per cent. Released time off school property for religious instruction is permitted, in the absence of stated board policy, in 22 school corporations, or 10 per cent. The large majority, 152, or 69.1 per cent, of the responding schools have no established policy but nevertheless do not participate in released-time programs off school property.

In response to the question concerning released time on school property for religious instruction, 27, or 12.7 per cent, of the respondents indicated that board policy prohibits the practice in their corporations. The policy of four school boards, or 1.9 per cent, permits the practice, and fourteen other respondents, or 6.6 per cent, noted that it is practiced in the absence of any definite policy. School board policy in one school corporation requires that pupils be released for religious instruction during the school day on school property. The large majority of the respondents, 166, or 78.3 per cent, stated that in the absence of policy released time for religious instruction on school property is not practiced in their school corporations.

The participants were asked if there is a shared-time program in effect in their school corporation, in which pupils from parochial schools attend one or more classes in the public schools. Fourteen school corporations, or 6.5 per cent, responded in the affirmative. Six of these stated that parochial school pupils participate in the public school instrumental music program; five school corporations share their vocational programs, and two share physical education programs with parochial schools.

Distribution of Gideon Bibles. The participants were asked to respond to several questions concerning other practices. One of these questions concerned the distribution of Gideon Bibles.

Gideon Bibles are distributed in 176, or 80 per cent, of the responding school corporations. Forty-four respondents, or 20 per cent, reported that they do not follow this practice. Several of the respondents in school corporations which permit the distribution of Gideon Bibles commented that this practice occurs at the fourth, fifth, or sixth grade level.

Baccalaureate Services. Two hundred and eight respondents, or 94.6 per cent, reported that their school corporations hold Baccalaureate services. Such services are held on school property in 168 responding school corporations, or 76.4 per cent of the cases. The services are compulsory in 56, or 25.5 per cent of the responding corporations, and penalties for failure to attend are imposed in seventeen, or 7.7 per cent. Twelve respondents, or 5.4 per cent, reported that their corporations do not hold Baccalaureate services. Some of the comments on this practice are as follows:

> Our Baccalaureate is not a religious service. It is planned by the school, and a clergyman speaks. It is not in association with any church or churches in general.

> So far, a senior has never refused to attend. The high school chorus is required to attend along with the senior class to provide choral singing.

> Unexcused absence marks incomplete high school requirements.

> Students may be excused by the principal, and if so, no penalty; otherwise, the diploma insert is withheld until the matter is resolved.

> No one has asked to be excused, but a request would be granted.

> We rotate members of the ministerial association as speakers.

> Held in local church. Usually rotate year in year out.

> Handled by the ministerial association.

> These services were discontinued a few years ago. Each church is encouraged to conduct own services.

School Clubs. The persons receiving the questionnaire were also asked if certain school-sponsored clubs with faculty sponsors such as Hi-Y, Y-Teens, CYO (Catholic Youth Organization), or Youth for Christ are in existence in any of their high schools. Table VI shows the number of responding school corporations having school-sponsored Hi-Y, Y-Teens, CYO, or Youth for Christ clubs with faculty sponsors. A total of 125, or 55.1 per cent, of the respondents indicated that one or more of these clubs are in existence in their school corporations.

TABLE VI. NUMBER OF RESPONDING SCHOOL CORPORATIONS
HAVING SCHOOL-SPONSORED HI-Y, Y-TEENS, CYO, OR YOUTH
FOR CHRIST CLUBS WITH FACULTY SPONSORS

Hi-Y		*Y-Teens*		*CYO*		*Youth for Christ*	
No.	*%*	*No.*	*%*	*No.*	*%*	*No.*	*%*
100	44.0	60	26.4	14	6.2	14	6.2

One hundred, or 44 per cent, of the respondents indicated that they have a Hi-Y club; sixty, or 26.4 per cent, have Y-Teens; fourteen, or 6.2 per cent have CYO; and fourteen, or 6.2 per cent, have Youth for Christ clubs in their schools. One respondent replied: "Students of all faiths belong to it [Hi-Y] freely." Another stated: "The high school has a Bible Club."

Use of school facilities by religious groups. In response to a question concerning the use of public school playground and/or athletic fields by religious groups, parochial schools, churches, or such organizations as Youth for Christ, Y-Teens, etc., 86, or 39.8 per cent of the respondents, indicated that such use was made; 130, or 60.2 per cent, indicated no such use. Thirty-three, or 38.4 per cent of those permitting such use, stated that a rental fee is charged. Several commented that the school playground is used by students at the vacation Bible school. A number of respondents noted that public school athletic fields are rented to parochial schools for athletic events such as football, baseball, and track.

In response to a question concerning the use of school buildings by such groups as those indicated above, 88 respondents, or 40.7 per cent, replied in the affirmative. One hundred twenty-eight, or 59.3 per cent, indicated no such use. The respondents in 24 school corporations, or 27.2 per cent of those permitting such use, stated that a rental fee is charged for use of school buildings by religious groups. The school gymnasium was most frequently mentioned as the building facility used. Several of the respondents commented that their corporations permit the use of public school buildings and facilities for summer vacation Bible school and by churches during building or remodeling programs.

Transportation of parochial pupils. The participants were asked if their corporations had purchased any extra buses or contracted for additional buses in order to transport parochial pupils. Thirteen, or 6.1 per cent, responded in the affirmative; 200, or 93.9 per cent, answered in the negative.

The participation of ministers, priests, and/or rabbis in school assembly programs. The respondents were asked whether ministers, priests, and/or rabbis speak at public school assembly programs on topics of a religious nature. One hundred forty-nine, or 66.5 per cent, reported in the affirmative; 75, or 33.5 per cent, answered in the negative. Numerous comments were made by the respondents concerning this practice. The comment most frequently made was that this practice occurs at Thanksgiving, Christmas, Easter. One respondent reported that "One day each month a convocation of a religious nature is held; a text is frequently read from the Bible."

Several who responded to this question stated that attendance is optional. One said, "No indoctrination." Another defended the practice with this statement: "We do not mention anything about a denomination or the characteristics of same." One respondent said these are "general inspirational talks." Several respondents remarked that the local ministerial society assigns the ministers or priests to these programs. Other comments were:

> We have one week set aside for Religious Emphasis Week.

> The ministers of the community plan special convocation programs for each day of the week.

> They speak only on topics considered within the law.

> Weekly worship service in one school. Monthly convocation in the high school by local ministers.

> I hope we have the courage to continue many of these things that have inspired man to be a strong moral person. Some of the complaints we hear are ridiculous.

The final question asked of the participants was as follows: "Has your school corporation made any change in policy regarding religion and the public schools as a result of either or both of the recent Supreme Court decisions relative to prayer and Bible reading?"

The respondents in twelve school corporations, or 5.5 per cent, responded that a change in policy had been made; 205, or 94.5 per cent, said that there had been no policy change.

Several participants responded that no board action had been taken but that school authorities were considerably more cautious concerning these activities. Typical comments were: "Caution in action" and "Teachers may continue as they desire—on their own—no policy from the board." One respondent commented: "Why bring it up? When, so far, we have had no problem." Another stated: "We surely will not [take board action] either, unless undue pressure is exerted."

Several other comments noted on the questionnaires reflect various attitudes toward the entire problem of religion and the public schools:

> I am greatly disturbed to think that we as school men should ever allow a small minority to take beauty such as this away from our boys and girls.

> I do not feel that this problem should be agitated.

> Certainly our basic foundations include freedom to practice or refrain from practicing certain religious concepts and conventions.

> The way I interpret this is that school boards, state, etc., cannot prescribe a certain religious prayer. I feel that the teacher, on her own volition, may use religious readings, prayers, etc., as long as it is not offensive to a child. In that event, I think the child can be excluded for that portion that is offensive to him. We plan to continue until *forced* to stop.

> I believe in freedom to worship as we please. I also believe it is wise to set an example approving freedom of worship. I hope we will not let the communists dominate us until we can not worship God.

Summary

Of the 264 questionnaires mailed to Indiana public school superintendents, there were 227, or 86 per cent, usable returns.

Responses of the participants which indicated definite school board policy in the area of religious practices in the schools were relatively few in number. The returns show a lack of written or formally stated board policy in Indiana public schools requiring, prohibiting, or permitting certain practices which might be considered to be religious in nature.

An analysis of the principal findings reveals the following:

1. Reading the Bible at the opening of the school day is permitted or practiced in approximately one-third of the responding school corporations.

2. The use of the Bible in the teaching of literature is permitted or practiced in nearly two-thirds of the responding school corporations.

3. Reciting the Lord's Prayer is permitted or practiced in nearly half of the responding school corporations.

4. Reciting a prescribed prayer is permitted or practiced in approximately one-fifth of the responding school corporations.

5. Prayer led by a pupil or teacher is permitted or practiced in approximately three-fifths of the responding school corporations. This practice was mentioned as occurring most often with the noon meal.

6. The singing of religious hymns is permitted or practiced in approximately two-thirds of the responding school corporations.

7. The singing of Christmas carols is permitted or practiced in all of the responding school corporations.

8. The use of Nativity scenes is permitted or practiced in over 90 per cent of the responding school corporations.

9. Released time for religious instruction away from school during the school day is required, permitted, or practiced in approximately one-fourth of the responding school corporations.

10. Released time for religious instruction on school property during the school day is required, permitted, or practiced in nearly ten per cent of the responding school corporations.

11. Shared-time programs are in effect in less than 10 per cent

of the responding school corporations, and even in these corporations, the shared-time program is quite limited in scope.

12. Less than five per cent of the school corporations reported that they teach a course in the Bible for credit. Only two school corporations reported a course in comparative religion.

13. The Gideon Society distributed Bibles in four-fifths of the responding school corporations.

14. Baccalaureate services are held in approximately 95 per cent of the responding school corporations. In over 75 per cent of the school corporations, these services are held on school property. In over 25 per cent the services are compulsory.

15. School clubs of a religious nature are sponsored by a school faculty member and meet on school property during the school day in over one half of the responding school corporations. Clubs most frequently named are Hi-Y and Y-Teens.

16. School buildings, playgrounds, and facilities are used by religious groups in approximately two-fifths of the responding school corporations. In approximately one-third of these situations a rental fee is required.

17. Few school corporations reported that extra school buses have been purchased or additional buses contracted in order to transport parochial pupils; however, several commented that they could get along with fewer buses if parochial pupils were not transported by the public schools.

18. The participation of ministers, priests, and/or rabbis in school assembly programs or convocations was reported by approximately two-thirds of the responding school corporations. These programs most often occur at Thanksgiving, Christmas, and Easter; however, several of the respondents

reported that they hold weekly or monthly assemblies where the clergy are invited to speak.

19. Less than 6 per cent of the responding school corporations reported a change in school board policy as a result of the recent Supreme Court decisions relative to prayer and Bible reading.

SELECTED BIBLIOGRAPHY

If you pursue the study of the problems of religion and education, the following books should prove valuable:

Benson, Purnell Handy. *Religion in Contempory Culture.* Harper and Brothers, New York, 1960.

Blanshard, Paul. *Religion and the Schools: The Great Controversy.* Beacon Press, Boston, 1963.

Boles, Donald E. *The Bible, Religion and the Public Schools.* (Second Edition), Iowa State University Press, Ames, Iowa, 1963.

Church, State and the Public Schools. Institute of Human Relations Press, American Jewish Committee, 165 E. 56th St., New York, 1963.

Culver, Raymond B. *Horace Mann and Religion in the Massachusetts Public Schools.* Yale University Press, New Haven, Conn., 1929.

Dewey, John. *A Common Faith.* Yale University Press, New Haven Conn., 1960 (Rev.).

Dierenfield, Richard B. *Religion in American Public Schools.* Public Affairs Press, Washington, D.C., 1962.

Drinan, Robert F. *Religion, The Courts and Public Policy,* McGraw-Hill, New York, 1963.

Drouin, Edmond G. *The School Question: A Bibliography on Church-State Relationships in American Education, 1940-1960.* Catholic University Press of America, Washington, D.C., 1963.

Fellman, David. *The Supreme Court and Education* (Classics in

Education, No. 4). Bureau of Publications, Teachers College, Columbia University, New York, 1960.

Frommer, Arthur. *The Bible and the Public Schools*. Liberal Press, Pocket Books, Inc., New York, 1963.

Hay, C. L. *The Blind Spot in American Public Education*. Macmillan, New York, 1950.

Healey, Robert M. *Jefferson on Religion in Public Education*. Yale University Press, New Haven, Conn., 1962.

Johnson, F. Ernest. *American Education and Religion: The Problems of Religion in the Schools*. Harper and Brothers, New York, 1952.

LaNoue, George. "The Supreme Court's New Frontier Between Religion and the Public Schools," *Phi Delta Kappan*, Volume XLV, No. 3, December, 1963.

McDowell, John B. and Powell, Theodore. *Religion and Education*. National Conference of Christians and Jews, 43 W. 57th St., New York, 1962.

Niebuhr, Reinhold. "Varieties of Religious Revival." *The New Republic*, June 6, 1955.

Oaks, Dallin H. *The Wall Between Church and State*. University of Chicago Press, Chicago, 1963.

O'Neill, James. *The Catholic in Secular Education*. Longmans, Green, 1956.

Rogers, Virgil M. "Are the Public Schools Godless?" *The Christian Century*, September 11, 1957.

Stokes, A. P. *Church and State in the United States*. Harper and Brothers, New York, 1950.

Thayer, V. T. *Religion in Public Education*. Viking Press, New York, 1947.

―――― *The Attack Upon the American Secular School*. Beacon Press, Boston, Mass., 1951.

Tussman, Joseph. *The Supreme Court and Church and State*. Oxford University Press, New York, 1962.

Van Egmond, Elmer. "Social Policy and Education," *Review of Educational Research*, Chapter VI, February, 1964, p. 15.

NOTES

CHAPTER ONE

1. *West Virginia Board of Education* v. *Barnette*, 319 U.S. 624, 63 S.Ct. 1178, 1186, 87 L.Ed. 1628.
2. *McCollum* v. *Board of Education of Champaign County, Illinois*, 333 U.S. 203, 68 S.Ct. 461, 92 L.Ed. 648, Z ALR 2d 1338.

CHAPTER THREE

1. *Everson* v. *Board of Education*, 330 U.S. 1, 67 S.Ct. 504, 91 L.Ed. 711, 168 A, L.R. 1392.
2. *McCollum* v. *Board of Education of Champaign County, Illinois*, 333 U.S. 203, 68 S.Ct. 461, 92 L.Ed. 648, Z ALR 2d 1338.
3. *Zorach* v. *Clauson*, 343 U.S. 306, 72 S.Ct. 670, 92, L.Ed. 954.
4. *Engel* v. *Vitale*, 370 U.S. 421, 82 S.Ct. 1261, 8 L.Ed. 2d, 601, 86 ALR 2d, 1285.
5. *School District of Abington Township, Pennsylvania* v. *Schempp*, 374 U.S. 203, 10 L.Ed. 2d 844, 83 S.Ct. 1560.
6. *Murray* v. *Curlett*, 374 U.S. 203, 10 L.Ed. 2d 844, 83 S.Ct. 1560.
7. *Chamberlain* v. *The Dade County Board of Instruction*, 374 U.S. 487, 10 L.Ed. 2d 1043, 83 S.Ct. 1864—Remanded to Supreme Court of Florida for further consideration. Subsequent opinion and decision 377 U.S. 402, 12 L.Ed. 2d 407, 84 S.Ct. 1272.

CHAPTER FOUR

1. Sherman Smith, *The Relation of the State to Religious Education* (New York: Syracuse University, 1926), p. 71.
2. M. G. Hunt, "Bible Study in Public Schools," *Peabody Journal of Education*, 23 (November, 1956), 156.
3. Ibid.
4. *"Time* Essay," *Time* Magazine, Vol. 85 (April 30, 1965), p. 44.

CHAPTER FIVE

1. Board of Christian Education of the Presbyterian Church in the United States of America, *The Church and the Public Schools* (Philadelphia, 1957), p. 10.
2. See Chapter 9 for a discussion of alternate choices in teaching about religion.
3. *The Church and the Public Schools*, p. 13.

CHAPTER SIX

1. Two recent books representing the Lutheran view are Albert G. Huegli, ed., *Church and State Under God* (St. Louis, Missouri: Concordia, 1964); and The Board of Social Ministry, Lutheran Church in America, *Church and State, A Lutheran Perspective* (New York, 1963).
2. Matthew, 28:19, 20, R.S.V.
3. Ephesians, 6:4, R.S.V.
4. *City of Louisville* v. *Commonwealth*, 134 Ky. 488, 121 S.W. 411.
5. Martin A. Haendschke, *The Sunday School Story* (River Forest, Illinois: Lutheran Education Association, 1963), pp. 109-115.
6. The variety of Lutheran weekday programs is described by Erich H. Kiehl, Bulletin 135, *The Weekday School* (St. Louis, Missouri: Board of Parish Education, The Lutheran Church-Missouri Synod).
7. Fred F. Beach and Robert F. Will, *The State and Non-Public Schools* (Washington: U.S. Government Printing Office, 1958), p. 1.

8. Educational Policies Commission, *Moral and Spiritual Values in the Public Schools* (Washington, D.C.: National Education Association, 1951).

9. American Council on Education, *The Relation of Religion to Public Education* (Washington, 1947).

10. National Council of Churches of Christ in the U.S.A., *Relation of Religion to Public Education* (New York, 1960).

11. Lutheran Church-Missouri Synod, *Proceedings of the 1953 Convention of the Lutheran Church-Missouri Synod* (St. Louis, Missouri: Lutheran Board of Parish Education, 1953).

12. Lutheran Board of Parish Education, *Parish Education Bulletin* (St. Louis, Missouri: The Lutheran Church-Missouri Synod, 1964), p. 3.

13. Lutheran Church-Missouri Synod, *Proceedings of the Forty-Third Convention of the Lutheran Church-Missouri Synod* (St. Louis, Missouri: Lutheran Church-Missouri Synod, 1956), p. 307.

14. Beach and Will, *The State and Non-Public Schools*, p. 1.

15. Lutheran Church-Missouri Synod, *Proceedings of the Forty-Fifth Regular Convention of the Lutheran Church-Missouri Synod* (St. Louis, Missouri: Lutheran Church-Missouri Synod, 1958), pp. 117-118.

16. *Proceedings* of 1965 Convention of The Lutheran Church-Missouri Synod, pp. 153-154.

17. George R. LaNoue, *Public Funds for Parochial Schools?* (New York: National Council of Churches of Christ in the U.S.A., 1963), pp. 22-23.

18. Ibid., p. 24.

19. Ibid., pp. 25-28.

CHAPTER SEVEN

1. See Chapter 3 for a discussion of related court decisions.

2. Leo Pfeffer, *Church, State and Freedom,* (Boston: Beacon Press, 1953), p. 476.

CHAPTER EIGHT

1. Eugene B. Borowitz, *Philosophies of Education*, Philip Phenix, ed. (New York: Wiley, 1963), p. 87.

2. Ibid., p. 88.

3. *Sabbath*, 31b.

4. *Sanhedrin*, 91a-b.

5. Martin Buber, *Hasidism* (New York: Philosophical Library, 1948), p. 135.

6. Joseph ben Judah ibn Aknin, *Cure of Souls* (12 Century), Chapter 27. Ibn Aknin's criteria for successful teaching may interest the modern reader: the teacher must have complete command of the subject he wishes to transmit; he must carry out in his own life the principles he wishes to inculcate in his pupils; he must exact no pay for his teaching; he must look upon his pupils as if they were his own sons; he must train his pupils to lead an ethical life; he must not be impatient but come to his pupils with a happy countenance; and he must teach his pupils according to the range of their intellectual capacities.

7. Moses Maimonides, *The Guide of the Perplexed*, Part I, Chapter 55. Cf. *Sabbath*, 75a.

8. Levi ben Gerson (Gersonides) in *The Wars of the Lord*, quoted by W. Gunther Plaut, *Judaism and the Scientific Spirit* (New York: Union of American Hebrew Congregations, 1962), p. 6. His books offers a superb exposition of the problem under discussion.

9. Ecclesiastes 12:13.

10. *Union Prayer Book*, Part I (Cincinnati: Central Conference of American Rabbis, 1940), p. 34.

11. Isaiah, 11:9.

12. Leo Pfeffer, *Creeds in Competition* (New York: Harper and Brothers, 1958), p. 60.

13. Eugene B. Borowitz, p. 93. Also, Anson Phelps Stokes and Leo Pfeffer, *Church and State in the United States* (New York: Harper and Row, 1964), p. 355.

14. Jews never acquiesced in lower court rulings which held the Lord's Prayer to be "non-denominational." Although the words, when taken literally, are not at variance with Jewish teaching, sacred usage over many centuries by Christians has made this prayer wholly Christian. As such, it violates the conscience of the Jew. The Lord to which the prayer's title refers is not God as Jews conceive of Him, but Jesus of the Christian tradition. Indeed, the words are the words of Jesus drawn verbatim from the Gospels.

15. Paul Tillich, *The Courage to Be* (New Haven: Yale University Press, 1952), pp. 182-184.

16. *Why the Bible Should Not be Read in the Public Schools,* pamphlet issued by the Central Conference of American Rabbis.

17. *Statement of the Commission on Social Action of Reform Judaism* to the Senate Judiciary Committee on October 3, 1962, opposing several resolutions which sought to modify the first amendment. Submitted by Rabbi Richard G. Hirsch.

18. Marvin Braiterman, *Religion and the Public Schools* (New York: Union of American Hebrew Congregations, 1958), pp. 25-26.

19. Rabbi Morris Adler, "Religion and Public Education: A Rationale," *Journal of the Central Conference of American Rabbis,* (April, 1955).

20. *American Council on Education Studies* (April, 1947), Vol. XI, No. 26, p. 19.

21. An unlikely happenstance. Agreement is difficult to reach. In New York City, for instance, representatives of the Protestant Council, the Roman Catholic Archdiocese and the Board of Rabbis met for many months of painstaking study only to conclude that agreement was hopeless.

22. Reinhold Niebuhr, quoted by Rabbi Morris Adler, "Religion and Public Education."

23. *Safeguarding Religious Liberty,* Position Paper issued by the Synagogue Council of America and the National Community Relations Advisory Council, through its Joint Advisory Committee (October, 1962), p. 7.

24. Ibid., pp. 4, 7.

25. Stokes and Pfeffer, p. 355.

26. Rabbi Maurice N. Eisendrath, President of the Union of American Hebrew Congregations, in testimony before the House Judiciary Committee, May 12, 1964.

27. In their classic exposition of Judaism's approach to the major social issues of our time, Albert Vorspan and Eugene J. Lipman suggest that the church's dissatisfaction with its own religious education efforts is primarily responsible for pressures urging the religionizing of the public school. See their *Justice and Judaism* (New York: Union of American Hebrew Congregations, 1959), pp. 51-52.

28. Rabbi Morris Adler, "Religion and Public Education."

CHAPTER NINE

1. Educational Policies Commission, *Moral and Spiritual Values in the Public Schools* (Washington, D.C.: National Education Association, 1951), pp. 77-78.
2. William B. Ball, "Of Schema, Hotheads, Theology and Smoke," *Teachers College Record*, Vol. 64 (February, 1963), p. 21.
3. *Moral and Spiritual Values in the Public Schools*, p. 72.
4. Ibid., pp. 72-73.

CHAPTER ELEVEN

1. For a discussion of court cases, see Chapter 3.

CHAPTER TWELVE

1. Mary Perkins Ryan, *Are Parochial Schools the Answer?* (New York: Holt, Rinehart and Winston, 1964).
2. Neil G. McCluskey, "Catholic Education: A Changing Pattern," *The Commonweal*, Vol. 79 (January 1964), p. 511.
3. The case for this commitment is ably stated by Monsignor O'Neil D'Amour in the January 31, 1964 issue of *The Commonweal*.
4. Eberhard Müller, *A New Road in Germany: Evangelical Academy* (Goppingen: Zeitungsverlag und Druckhaus GmbH., 1955), p. 1.
5. Supreme Court of the United States, Nos. 142 and 119, October Term, 1963, p. 72.
6. National Council of Churches, *The Churches and the Public Schools* (New York: The National Council of Churches, June 1963), p. 13.5-1.
7. Ibid., p. 13.5-2.
8. Educational Policies Commission, *Moral and Spiritual Values in the Public Schools* (Washington, D.C.: National Education Association, 1951), p. 27.
9. Alfred North Whitehead, *The Aims of Education and Other Essays*, (New York: Macmillan, 1929), p. 27.
10. Heinz-Dietrich Wendland, *Die Kirche in der Modernen Gesellschaft* (Hamburg: Furche-Verlag, 1956), p. 14.

11. Klaus von Bismarck, Address at the Assembly of the World Council of Churches, New Delhi, November 1961.

12. Molly Batten, Address at the Assembly of the World Council of Churches, New Delhi, November 1961.

13. V. K. Matthew, Address at the Assembly of the World Council of Churches, New Delhi, November 1961.